Government Relations

for Canadian Associations

How to Be the Voice of your Members with Government

Huw Williams

3rd Edition

Published by
Canadian Society of Association Executives
10 King Street East, Suite 1100
Toronto, Ontario M5C 1C3
www.csae.com

Library and Archives Canada Cataloguing in Publication

Williams, Huw, 1966-
     Government relations for Canadian associations : how to be the voice of
     your members with government / Huw Williams. — 3rd ed.

     Previously published under title: Guide to government relations for
     directors of not-for-profit organizations.

ISBN 978-0-9811910-6-5

     1. Lobbying—Canada. 2. Advocacy advertising—Canada. 3. Associations,
     institutions, etc.—Political activity—Canada. 4. Nonprofit organizations—
     Political activity—Canada. I. Williams, Huw, 1966- . Guide to government
     relations for directors of not-for-profit organizations II. Canadian Society
     of Association Executives II. Title.

JL148.5.W55 2010   324'.40971   C2010-907834-9

Printed in Canada

CANADIAN SOCIETY OF ASSOCIATION EXECUTIVES
          SOCIÉTÉ CANADIENNE DES DIRECTEURS D'ASSOCIATION

Table of Contents

Preface

I have worked in the most senior levels of government in several jurisdictions, and seen lobbying at its worst and at its best. I have seen hit-and-run lobbying that fails because it lacks basic follow-up. I have seen rude, ill-informed lobbyists do more harm than good to their members. On the positive side, I have seen the most effective association lobbyists become invaluable resources on tough policy issues.

I have also worked as the in-house government relations director for one of Canada's largest associations, so I know the pressures and demands placed on association staff. I understand the complexities of board dynamics. Most recently, I have spent the last 15 years as a consultant to a wide variety of Canada's leading associations.

This book, therefore, represents the combined experience of numerous associations that embarked on a wide variety of advocacy campaigns at all levels of government. The backbone of this project is the analysis of these efforts—and the distillation of practices and approaches that work and, of course, of those that do not work.

Many well-respected association board members and senior staff members were interviewed for this project. Their wisdom and knowledge proved invaluable in preparing this book.

Huw Williams

Acknowledgements

With thanks and appreciation to all those individuals who helped make this guide a reality. First, to all the great association clients who I have been privileged to work with over the years, thank you. The experience of helping association leaders solve real issues and break through to government decision makers is the foundation of this book. Being a trusted advisor to an association leader is a privilege I am thankful for every day. Yes, sometimes that means emergency calls late at night or on weekends, but the bottom line is that it is an honour to be considered an insider to an association leadership. A special thanks to Rick Gauthier, for becoming our first client and being with us all the way over the last 14 years.

To every team member at Impact Public Affairs, thank you for your invaluable work and contributions. Each member of our team takes problem solving personally in a way that is more than a job; it is a passion. As a result we are more than a team at Impact.

I would like to thank the team at the Canadian Society of Association Executives for believing in this publication. The volunteer board of CSAE ensures that the society is a special place for shared learning and peer collaboration. CEO Michael Anderson ensures that the staff sets the bar high in every endeavour and I hope we lived up to that in this book.

Thank you to Bob Hamp and Dave Cybak at CSAE, who were pivotal in launching this project. Finally and most importantly, I would like to thank Jennifer Iveson, publications manager at CSAE. She more than anyone pushed this guide in a direction that included the most up-to-date content and spirit. She also redefined patience it what was a very hectic year.

Thank you!

About the New Edition

This book is a new and refocused edition of my earlier book with CSAE, *A Guide to Government Relations for Directors of Not-for-Profit Organizations*. A fresh look is needed now for several reasons.

First, the political atmosphere surrounding lobbying has changed radically over the last decade. Governments now demand full transparency of lobbying objectives and activities. There is increasing skepticism among elected politicians that lobbyists are credible and legitimate. More and more elected leaders question whether associations are trustworthy participants in the legislative process. Understanding this dynamic—and overcoming it with best practices—are important objectives of this work.

Second, the rules governing lobbying have tightened significantly at all levels of government. This book aims to underscore the importance of understanding and following those rules. It highlights proper lobby registration conduct as a core new responsibility for association staff and senior staff officers.

Third, rapidly evolving technology has had a huge impact on shaping public policy. Researching government policy, posting association advocacy positions, and mobilizing members can happen much faster and the implications for association advocacy are huge.

Finally, the advocacy environment has become more competitive than ever. Gaining and maintaining the attention of decision makers is more difficult than ever.

Associations that do not follow a proactive and well-guided approach to government relations risk being left behind.

This book attempts to ensure its readers are on the cutting edge of lobbying and can break through the clutter and deliver their members' message with success.

Since the last edition there have been major changes in the Canadian government relations world. These changes influence almost every aspect of how associations lobby government. Legislative and regulatory initiatives have spearheaded changes that require greater transparency for associations working with government. This book covers the new world of lobbying rules that require associations not only to disclose what they lobby for, but also to whom, when, and how they lobby. These rule changes are critical for association staff and board members to understand. These rule changes have had an impact on the perception of lobbying and have sometimes made it more difficult to reach decision makers. As a result, sound and creative advocacy strategies are needed now more than ever. This book elaborates in greater detail the principles for lobbying success and case studies of association victories. Finally, rapidly changing online advances are continuing to shape how advocacy and indeed how democracies work. Advocacy and the online world are in this new edition.

Introduction

Introduction

Associations form to enable individuals, or similar businesses, to achieve common goals. Government relations activities undertaken by associations provide members with a greater voice in government decision making, and ultimately protect member interests. When dealing with the increasingly complex world of government regulation and legislation, it makes sense that collective action has a far greater chance of getting tangible results.

Historically, many associations were formed to deal primarily with advocacy issues. Today, even more associations have taken on government relations responsibilities as the ever-increasing reach of government affects the concerns of individuals and not-for-profit organizations. Whether the purpose of the association is to represent individuals, professionals, or business-based concerns, a formal government relations approach is more necessary than ever.

Canadian association research demonstrates that government relations is the most important activity for most membership-based organizations. Indeed, over 90 per cent of Canadian associations are engaged in government relations at some level. Yet research on the subject also reveals that associations do not commit enough resources to fulfilling this mandate, and in many cases associations have not determined the best approach to achieve success.[1]

1.   Belfall, Donald, *Associations in Canada, Future Impact and Influence*, Toronto, O◀ Foundation for Association Research and Education, 1995.

The goal of this book is to help association executives and board members better understand the elements necessary to achieve success in government relations.

Who This Book Is For

This book is designed for association staff and board members who need to engage government to resolve member issues. The objective is to provide readers with a straightforward explanation of how to achieve results when dealing with government.

The predominant viewpoint of this book is that a proactive and well-thought-out government relations strategy best serves the needs of association members. A fundamental principle for any association to be successful in dealing with government is to develop relationships with policy makers before a crisis takes place.

As I hope to demonstrate, the best advocacy approach involves educating and sensitizing decision makers over time. Associations are strongly advised to position themselves as a resource to government-policy decision makers. This single action ensures long-term success in the government relations arena. This is a book of action, not a civics guide to government. It is a tactical guide for achieving association lobby goals—at all levels of Canadian government relations. It provides a road map for association staff and board members starting out in government relations and an insight for experienced professionals to take their efforts to a higher level.

Government Relations in Three Parts

Part one, "Preparing Your Association," covers the elements that make a good advocacy foundation for any association. It covers the important rules and regulations that govern modern-day lobbying. It highlights the critical senior-staff responsibility and accountability for lobbying registration and disclosure. This part also sets the foundations for good strategic advocacy planning.

Part two, "Delivering Your Message to Government," provides insight into working with senior government officials and their elected counterparts. Insight into how political offices are staffed and what approaches work best is outlined. It also highlights how to deal with important legislative committees.

Part three, "Completing the Advocacy Picture," looks at the remaining pieces of a successful advocacy campaign. A separate chapter on media and its impact on the political process, and one on the importance of grassroots advocacy, are in this section. Issues around conducting research, forming coalitions, and working with a minority government are also examined.

Government Relations, Lobbying and Advocacy: Do They Mean the Same?

Yes and no. Throughout this book the terms will be used interchangeably in much the same way they are used in the government relations profession on a day-to-day basis. However, you should remember that lobbying is a loaded word, with connotations of too much influence or pressure. Advocacy is often used in its place because it conveys a more subtle and sometimes softer means of changing government policy.

Associations and Government

Government officials and politicians generally have limited working knowledge of, or practical experience with, the industries for which they develop policy. Too often, association members assume that their working world is well understood by outsiders and more particularly by the policy makers that govern them. This is a dangerous assumption.

Compounding this dilemma, the current political landscape has thousands of interest groups competing for limited government resources; decision makers are constantly shifting their focus from one issue to another. Interest groups need to be more proactive to gain government attention or they risk being marginalized.

In establishing a government relations program, by their very nature associations are uniquely positioned for three reasons:

1. They can draw on the practical expertise of the board and membership.

2. They can effectively focus discussions and policy debate with governments—it is easier to speak with and negotiate with one association than with multiple individuals.

3. They tend to have a broad grassroots membership base to which governments are prone to listen.

The larger the constituency, the harder it is for elected officials or government policy makers to ignore. As a result, associations are well positioned to be very effective at government relations. They have the wisdom and experience of many successful managers, and they have the members to execute the message.

From a government's perspective, associations bring a multitude of benefits:

1. It is easier to communicate with one association than 100 individual constituents.

2. Associations can help build consensus; associations can provide governments with practical experiences and advice.

3. Associations can provide a cost-effective partnership for administering government policy.

However, associations must understand the motivations and constraints of government, and always consider the government's own agenda when embarking on advocacy activity. Successful government relations strategies fit into the government's agenda or find arguments that support major policy pronouncements, such as the Speech from the Throne, budgets, and major policy papers. Associations must also understand the plans and priorities of various government departments to be successful in advancing an advocacy agenda. Advocacy efforts that are closely aligned with the government's own agenda are most likely to succeed.

The Role of the Association Senior Staff

Government relations facilitates a two-way dialogue between an organization and a level of government. The role of management is to examine what is going on in and around government, communicate that to members, and counsel the board on how to respond. The association's role is then to take the industry back to government.

It is important for associations to consider the assignment of responsibility for government relations activities. Overall, my experience with Canadian associations demonstrates that about 40 per cent of associations have full-time government relations staff. Larger associations have assigned staff to manage government relations; however, smaller groups tend not to have the financial resources to employ a dedicated government relations manager.

One of the most fundamental decisions an association must make is the extent to which government relations responsibilities are assigned to the association's senior staff officer. Based on my experience, there is a continuing trend among Canadian associations to ensure that the most senior association staff officer maintain primary responsibility for government relations.

In these cases, the association's chief staff officer (CSO) serves as the voice of the association to government, and maintains overall strategic responsibility for directing the association's advocacy efforts. This trend holds true even among those associations with assigned full-time government relations staff. The principle behind this trend is the increasing realization of the importance of advocacy to association members. My experience has demonstrated that associations are more successful at advocacy when the CSO remains directly engaged in government relations.

> **TIP FROM THE TRENCHES:**
> **Chief Staff Officer Involvement**
>
> Randy Williams, president of the Tourism Industry Association of Canada and a frequent public speaker on association leadership, highlights the importance of the CSO (or CEO) taking an active role in government relations: "Association CEOs cannot remove themselves from advocacy planning and implementation. Most association members place a great deal of emphasis on government relations issues and they expect senior level attention, decision making and focus on advocacy. Even if your organization has senior government relations staff, the CEO must take a leadership role and be directly involved in advocacy."

Preparing Your Association

Lobbying Rules and Registration

Chapter 1.

Lobbying Rules and Registration

No other aspect of lobbying and advocacy has changed more in the last decade than the need for transparency and accountability. All levels of government demand that associations lobby government on the public record and in ways that record advocacy objectives and tactics.

Most Canadian jurisdictions achieve transparency through public registries. The onus of registering to lobby in a given jurisdiction is on the association and must be taken seriously. In many jurisdictions, failure to register or update lobby activity is a criminal offence; ignorance of the law is never an excuse.

The first step for any advocacy effort is to review the advocacy rules for the level of government you are lobbying and make sure you follow registration guidelines and procedures. Those organizations already engaged in lobbying should periodically review registration procedures to ensure compliance.

The good news is that most jurisdictions make the lobbying registration process understandable and accessible. Following is a review of the federal system for registration and a full list of provincial and major municipalities that require lobby registration.[1]

---

1. The following section contains information taken from the Lobbying Act R.S., 1985, c. 44 (4th Supp.), s. 1; 2006, c. 9, s. 66 and related legal documents, all of which can be found online at **http://www.ocl-cal.gc.ca**. While all efforts were made to ensure accuracy at the time of printing, it is best to consult the original legislation and associated material published by the Office of the Commissioner of Lobbying of Canada at the above link.

Federal Lobbyist Registration and Rules

The federal government continues to play a leadership role in creating proactive lobbying registration systems and rules. Many of the recent changes have been driven by a political climate in Ottawa that sees lobbying as a potential source of scandal. (Most Canadians are familiar with the 2004 sponsorship scandal and the resulting Gomery Commission of Inquiry that led to specific recommendations to clean up Canada's lobbying and ethics rules.) As a result, the federal government has dramatically increased accountability for associations and private companies when it comes to lobbying rules and registration.

At the federal level, it is important to note that the onus for correct registration and disclosure of lobbying activities falls heavily on the shoulders of the association's chief staff officer (CSO). The rules make it clear that this is a personal responsibility and not one that can be delegated to subordinates. It is crucial that the CSO recognize his or her direct accountability and take steps to ensure compliance. Legal consequences for an association that fails to comply with the Act will land squarely on the CSO.

You can find the guide to federal registration at **http://www.ocl-cal.gc.ca**—the Office of the Commissioner of Lobbying of Canada. This site provides details for the *Lobbying Act*, regulations, the Code of Conduct, interpretation bulletins, and advisory opinions. All of these should be consulted in detail before lobbying at the federal level.

While this book includes a summary of key elements of the federal rules, the summary should not serve as a replacement for consulting the law

> **It is crucial that the CSO recognize his or her direct accountability and take steps to ensure compliance. Legal consequences for an association that fails to comply with the Act will land squarely on the CSO.**

Chapter 1.

Lobbying Rules and Registration

in detail or be construed as legal advice. Knowing and understanding the federal lobbying rules is one of the most important emerging responsibilities of any association engaged in lobbying at the federal level.

The federal lobbying website also provides a one-stop site for updating association information and lobbying objectives. It provides easy-to-use web-based registration for certain lobby activities. This site should be the go-to site for any association actively engaged in federal lobbying.

Basic Principles of the *Lobbying Act*

The guiding principle behind the federal *Lobbying Act* was to address public concerns that some people have more access than others to government decision makers, and consequently more ability to influence decisions. As a result, in 1988 Parliament established the *Lobbying Act* to contribute to confidence in the integrity of government decision making.

Subsequent Parliaments have introduced amendments to increase accountability, most notably in 1997, 2003, 2005. Significant changes were also introduced under the new *Federal Accountability Act* of 2006. These legislative changes represent a continuing trend of broad multi-party support for greater accountability in lobbying.

There are some important principles in the preamble to the *Lobbying Act* that are worth noting. These principles make it clear that lobbying is a legitimate activity and one that associations should proudly pursue. The *Act* seeks to make clear that increased registration and public accountability do not make lobbying less legitimate. These principles are:

- Free and open access to government is an important matter of public interest;
- Lobbying public office holders is a legitimate activity;

- It is desirable that public office holders and the public be able to know who is engaged in lobbying activities; and,

- The system for the registration of paid lobbyists should not impede free and open access to government.

As a starting point the *Lobbying Act* also makes clear what constitutes lobbying:

Lobbying is communicating with a public office holder for payment in respect of:

- The development of any legislative proposal;

- The introduction, defeat, or amendment of any Bill or resolution;

- The making or amendment of any regulation;

- The development or amendment of any policy or program;

- The awarding of any grant, contribution, or other financial benefit.

The definition of payment here is important. Association staff members are included because, in most cases, they work in paid positions.

Citizens complaining about levels of taxation or general government policy are not being paid and therefore have no need to register when contacting federal officials. Similarly, associations that are purely voluntary are exempt.

The *Act* provides for different categories of lobbyists: In-house (corporations and organizations) and Consultant. While it is important to understand that there are different rules for each category, most association leaders need only focus on the rules for In-house lobbyist. These are defined generally as a person who is employed by a not-for-profit entity such as a university, a charity or an association.

> **These principles make it clear that lobbying is a legitimate activity and one that associations should proudly pursue.**

Chapter 1.

Lobbying Rules and Registration

The entity is registered by its most senior officer as an organization that lobbies, if lobbying constitutes a significant part of the duties of one employee or would constitute a significant part of the duties of one employee if they were performed by only one employee.

The phrase "constitutes a significant part of duties of one employee" led to an important interpretation bulletin, *A Significant Part of Duties ("The 20 percent Rule"),* which establishes the threshold after which lobbying represents a significant part of one's duties has been established at 20 per cent or more of overall duties.

The officer responsible for filing the association's return must determine whether or not lobbying constitutes a significant part of the duties of the employees who communicate with public office holders and who are subject to the 20 per cent rule. This can be done using various approaches. One way is to estimate the time spent preparing for communicating (researching, drafting, planning, compiling, travelling, etc.) and actually communicating with public office holders. For example, a one-hour meeting may require seven hours of preparation and two hours of travel time. In this case, the time for lobbying is a total of 10 hours.

In situations where the time is difficult to estimate, the filing officer responsible must review all of the employee's duties and determine the proportion for lobbying activities. Both methods may be used in conjunction if the situation is unclear. In any case, the filing officer is accountable for the decision of whether or not registration is necessary.

The requirement to register is triggered for an association when the total amount of time spent lobbying by all paid employees equals 20 per cent or more of the working hours of one employee. As a baseline, this should be calculated on a monthly basis.

While this interpretation provides clarity on which associations must register and which associations are not lobbying enough to require registration, I strongly recommend that any association actively lobbying should err on the side of caution, contribute to transparency, and register. In other words, if your association comes anywhere near the 20 per cent threshold, register!

There are few advantages to not registering because your association is just under the threshold. One advantage could be that competing interest groups cannot check the lobbyist registration system to track and counteract your activities. In my opinion, this theoretical advantage is dwarfed by potential liability concerns—and the public criticism—that could accompany accusations of failing to register.

Associations registering to lobby are required to post online, and then publically make available, details such as:

- The names and addresses of the filing officer, employees, employer, organization, corporation or subsidiaries
- A summary of the employer's activities
- A description of the organization's membership
- Any government funding received
- The names of every employee whose duties involve lobbying
- Subject matters of the communications, and targeted departments
- Indications if employees were previous public office holders or designated public office holders, with details of their duties
- Communication techniques

The requirement for listing employees' previous positions as a federal public office holder or designated public office holder is there to ensure that

In other words, if your association comes anywhere near the 20 per cent threshold, register!

Chapter 1.

Lobbying Rules and Registration

past federal employees do not lobby the government inappropriately. It is important for associations to note that former federal employees face restrictions on when they can lobby the federal government and in what context. For example, former cabinet ministers cannot lobby government for five years after leaving their position. These restrictions are outlined in the Act and bear review if hiring a former federal employee on staff or as a consultant.

In 2010, the public case of former Member of Parliament (MP) Rahim Jaffer highlighted the importance of former federal employees understanding lobbying rules. In this case, the former Conservative caucus chair and long-time MP was pilloried by the media and forced to testify before a special parliamentary committee into his alleged unregistered lobbying activities. Jaffer was criticized by MPs from all parties for his conduct, and became a major national media story. Interestingly, the companies he worked with had little or no knowledge of federal lobbying rules and also came under intense media criticism. Jaffer's case is a cautionary tale to remind association leaders that potential breaches of the Lobbying Act can lead to unfavourable front page coverage for all involved.

Special Rules for Dealing with Designated Public Office Holders

The Lobbying Act contains special provisions for disclosure of contact with senior government officials defined as Designated Public Office Holders (DPOH). As lobbying rules are updated at the federal level they are posted online. Consult the website **http://www.ocl-cal.gc.ca** for details.

At the time of this book's printing the Lobbying Act defines in section 2(1) a DPOH as:

- A minister of the Crown or a minister of state and any person employed in his or her office who is appointed under subsection 128(1) of the Public Service Employment Act,

- Any other public office holder who, in a department within the meaning of paragraph (a), (a.1) or (d) of the definition "department" in section 2 of the *Financial Administration Act*:

    - Occupies the senior executive position, whether by the title of deputy minister, chief executive officer or by some other title, or

    - Is an associate deputy minister or an assistant deputy minister or occupies a position of comparable rank, and

- Any individual who occupies a position that has been designated by regulation under the provisions of the *Lobbying Act*.

There are 14 positions or classes of positions that associations should be aware of:

- Member of Parliament

- Member of Senate

- Any staff working in the offices of the Leader of the Opposition in the House of Commons or in the Senate

- Chief of the Defence Staff

- Vice Chief of the Defence Staff

- Chief of Maritime Staff

- Chief of Land Staff

- Chief of Air Staff

- Chief of Military Personnel

- Judge Advocate General

- Any positions of Senior Advisor to the Privy Council Office to which the office holder is appointed by the Governor in Council

- Deputy Minister (Inter-governmental Affairs) Privy Council Office

- Comptroller General of Canada

> " Jaffer's case is a cautionary tale to remind association leaders that potential breaches of the Lobbying Act are important and can lead to unfavourable front page coverage for all involved. "

Chapter 1.

Lobbying Rules and Registration

- Any position to which the office holder is appointed pursuant to paragraph 127.1(1)(a) or (b) of the *Public Employment Act*

Also, associations need to be aware of anyone holding a DPOH position on an acting basis. Associations are required to file a return monthly, updating the Lobbyist Registration system regarding communications with a DPOH. Details should include the name, position title and rank, the government institution involved, the date of the communication, and the subject matter of the communication. The Commissioner may verify the return content with the DPOH.

In addition to reporting meetings with a DPOH, associations are required to file updates on their advocacy activities no later than 15 days after the end of every month if:

- Information contained in an active return is no longer correct or additional information that the lobbyist has become aware of should be included in an active return,
- The lobbying activities have terminated or no longer require registration, or
- Five months have elapsed since the end of the last month in which a return was filed.

Penalties for Breaching the *Lobbying Act*

Penalties for association staff breaching the *Lobbying Act* are serious. They serve as a stark reminder of the importance of following the *Act* and of having a management plan in place to ensure the *Act* and its regulations are followed on an ongoing basis. The penalties are:

- Up to $50,000 and/or 6 months in jail on summary conviction
- Up to $200,000 and/or 2 years in jail on indictment

Reporting Government Funding

The federal *Lobbyists Registration Regulations* also require associations to report whether they receive funding from a domestic or foreign government or government agency.

Associations must publicly disclose:

- The end-date of the entity's last completed fiscal year,
- The dollar amount of funding received in the entity's last completed fiscal year,
- The name of the entity that is providing the funding, and
- Whether funding is expected in the entity's current financial year.

Lobbyists' Code of Conduct

One final area of federal lobbying responsibility that associations must be aware of and follow is the *Lobbyists' Code of Conduct* (the Code). The Code complements the registration requirements of the *Lobbying Act* and provides guidance for those dealing with government so that public trust can be maintained. Key elements of the *Lobbyists' Code of Conduct* are as follows.

Principles

Integrity and Honesty—Lobbyists should conduct with integrity and honesty all relations with public office holders, clients, employers, the public and other lobbyists.

Openness—Lobbyists should, at all times, be open and frank about their lobbying activities, while respecting confidentiality.

Professionalism—Lobbyists should observe the highest professional and ethical standards. In particular, lobbyists should conform fully with not only the letter but the spirit of the *Lobbyists' Code of Conduct* as well as all the relevant laws, including the *Lobbying Act* and its regulations.

Chapter 1.

Lobbying Rules and Registration

Rules

Transparency

Identity and purpose—Lobbyists shall, when making a representation to a public office holder, disclose the identity of the person or organization on whose behalf the representation is made, as well as the reasons for the approach.

Accurate information—Lobbyists shall provide information that is accurate and factual to public office holders. Moreover, lobbyists shall not knowingly mislead anyone and shall use proper care to avoid doing so inadvertently.

Disclosure of obligations—Lobbyists shall indicate to their client, employer or organization their obligations under the *Lobbying Act*, and their obligation to adhere to the *Lobbyists' Code of Conduct*.

Confidentiality

Confidential information—Lobbyists shall not divulge confidential information unless they have obtained the informed consent of their client, employer or organization, or disclosure is required by law.

Insider information—Lobbyists shall not use any confidential or other insider information obtained in the course of their lobbying activities to the disadvantage of their client, employer or organization.

Conflict of interest

Competing interests—Lobbyists shall not represent conflicting or competing interests without the informed consent of those whose interests are involved.

Disclosure—Consultant lobbyists shall advise public office holders that they have informed their clients of any actual, potential or apparent conflict of interest, and obtained the informed consent of each client concerned before proceeding or continuing with the undertaking.

Improper influence—Lobbyists shall not place public office holders in a conflict of interest by proposing or undertaking any action that would constitute an improper influence on a public office holder.

Breaches of the Code come under the purview of the Commissioner of Lobbying but carry different sanctions than breaches of the *Lobbying Act* registration requirements. There are no fines or jail sentences but the Commissioner must table investigation reports before both Houses of Parliament for public disclosure. Therefore, those breaching the Code will be publically highlighted in a negative way.

While the details of the federal lobbying provisions seem somewhat complicated on first review, they are well administered and made easier by a well-functioning online system. That said, association staff must be diligent to ensure the rules are followed and reports filed as required.

Provincial Government Lobbying Requirements

At the time of publication, only three provinces in Canada do not have provincial legislation governing lobbyist registration: Prince Edward Island, New Brunswick and Saskatchewan. All other provinces have provincial Lobbyist Registration Acts.

Province/Territory	PROVINCIAL LOBBYIST REGISTRATION REQUIRED	YEAR ENACTED (OR AMENDED)
Alberta	yes	2009
British Columbia	yes	2009
Manitoba	yes	pending
New Brunswick	no	
Newfoundland & Labrador	yes	2009
Northwest Territories	no	
Nova Scotia	yes	2007
Nunavut	no	
Ontario	yes	1999
Prince Edward Island	no	
Quebec	yes	2002
Saskatchewan	no	
Yukon	no	

Chapter 1.

Lobbying Rules and Registration

Ontario

The Lobbyists Registration Act, S.O.1998, c.27 came into force on January 15, 1999. This act creates a registration system for lobbyists that is almost identical to the system already established for the lobbying of federal officials under federal legislation.

Any individual or organization that lobbies to an official of the provincial government, or any Ontario board, agency or commission is now required to register with the Office of the Integrity Commissioner (the "Registrar"). Failure to file on time could result in a fine of up to $25,000.

- See http://www.elaws.gov.on.ca/html/statutes/english/elaws_statutes_98l27_e.htm for more information.

Quebec

In Quebec, lobbyists must declare particulars about their lobbying activities in a public registry. This declaration allows the public to find out who is attempting to influence which decisions of persons working within parliamentary, government and municipal institutions.

All lobbyists must abide by the following Acts:

- Lobbying Transparency and Ethics Act (last updated May 1, 2010) http://www2.publicationsduquebec.gouv.qc.ca/dynamicSearch/telecharge.php?type=2&file=%2F%2FT_11_011%2FT11_011_A.htm

- Code of Conduct for Lobbyists http://www2.publicationsduquebec.gouv.qc.ca/dynamicSearch/telecharge.php?type=3&file=/T_11_011/T11_011R0_2_A.HTM

British Columbia

The British Columbia Registrars now have investigative powers, and can impose fines upon lobbyists who violate the act or ban offenders from lobbying for up to two years. Refer to http://www.lobbyistsregistrar.bc.ca/ for details. And, check the following websites for more information:

- *Bill 20-2001: Lobbyists Registration Act: [SBC 2001]
  Chapter 42*
  http://www.leg.bc.ca/37th2nd/3rd_read/gov20-3.htm

- *Bill 19- 2009: Lobbyists Registration Amendment Act,
  2009* outlines all amendments made to original act
  http://www.leg.bc.ca/39th1st/1st_read/gov19-1.htm

Alberta

The Alberta legislation ensures that the public sees that
lobbying is done without a conflict of interest. Three
important features of the Bill are:

- Lobbyist registry that will give Albertans easy access to
  public information about who is paid to influence the
  government, and on what issues,

- An index of government contract information, and

- A ban on lobbying and providing advice to government
  on the same issue at the same time.

See the *Lobbyists Act: Chapter L-20.5* (current as of
September 28 2009) at the following website for more
information: http://www.qp.alberta.ca/570.cfm?frm_
isbn=9780779729647&search_by=link

Manitoba

The Lobbyist Registration for Manitoba has not yet been
implemented at the time of printing. The legislation to
create a formal system and new post for lobbyists was
passed in late 2008; however, the system is still not fully up
and running. See http://web2.gov.mb.ca/laws/statutes/2008/
c04308e.php for more information.

Nova Scotia

Nova Scotia passed the *Lobbyist Registration Act* on
November 8, 2001. Anyone who is paid to lobby a public
servant may need to register.

- A consultant must register within 10 days of being
  retained by a client.

Chapter 1.

Lobbying Rules and Registration

- Company employees who spend significant time lobbying must register within two months after becoming a lobbyist.

- The senior officer of an organization such as a professional association or society must register employees who spend significant time lobbying within two months after they become lobbyists.

All active registrations must be renewed every six months. Where required, updates such as address changes must be made within 30 days. *Bill No. 7 - An Act to Provide for the Registration of Lobbyists*, and the *Lobbyists' Registration Act: Chapter 34 of the Acts of 2001* can be found at **http://www.gov.ns.ca/lobbyist.**

Newfoundland and Labrador

A consultant lobbyist or an in-house lobbyist who lobbies a public office holder shall be registered in the registry of lobbyists with respect to those lobbying activities. A consultant lobbyist or in-house lobbyist shall not lobby a public office holder unless that person is registered in the registry of lobbyists with respect to those lobbying activities.

See the *Lobbyist Registration Act, Chapter L-24.1, SNL 2004* (most recent amendment in 2008) at **http://www.assembly.nl.ca/legislation/sr/statutes/l24-1.htm** for more information.

Major Municipalities and Lobbying Rules

A review of the ten largest municipalities in the country reveals an inconsistent approach. As of this book's publication, only the City of Toronto had a complete lobbyist registration system. Toronto is Canada's largest municipality and third largest overall government, so it is not surprising that its system emphasizes public disclosure of lobbying activities and regulation of lobbyists' conduct.

The city's main instrument for doing this is the Lobbyist Registry, which is an online, searchable tool that documents all lobbying activities in the City of Toronto. This system is backed up by the *Lobbying By-law* that was enacted by Toronto City Council in July 2008. These rules require lobbyists to report their lobbying activities within three business days after lobbying. Lobbyists must report the public office holder, subject matter, date of communication, and method of communication.

The City of Hamilton has established a Voluntary Lobbyist Registry as a public document. Lobbyists can voluntarily register by completing the city's Delegation Request Form, and the information is placed on a Registry that is available for public viewing in the Office of the City Clerk or online.

Other Ontario municipalities such as Ottawa are reviewing possible lobby registries as a result of the provincial legislation under the *Municipal Act* that now enables municipalities to implement mandatory lobbyist registries as of January 1, 2008.

Association staff should check directly with municipal staff to verify lobbying rules prior to conducting advocacy at this level. As public accountability on lobbying sweeps through higher levels of government, it is certain that municipalities will follow.

From a political optics perspective, it is recommended that even if a given jurisdiction does not have lobbying rules, associations are best served by using the federal rules and codes of conduct as a guiding principle. Lobbying behind closed doors is a thing of the past—associations that proactively respond to the transparency environment will be well served.

> **As public accountability on lobbying sweeps through higher levels of government, it is certain that municipalities will follow.**

Developing an Advocacy Strategy

Chapter 2.

Developing an Advocacy Strategy

Lobbying in Canada used to have an air of backroom deals or hidden influence. It was largely seen as something done behind the scenes by insiders, hidden from public view. The public perception of lobbyists was of fast operators who used their personal political connections to unfairly influence the outcome of government decisions. The 1980s (when Brian Mulroney was prime minister) were widely tainted with accusations and investigations surrounding inappropriate lobbying. The legacy of the airbus affair and subsequent revelations of cash payments for international lobbying was to leave many Canadians wondering about the extent and propriety of backroom lobbying.

Much has changed. Today, there is a growth of political professionalism; organizations must rely on building campaigns that are both proactive and subject to higher degrees of public scrutiny. No longer are problems solved with one phone call to a minister or one key meeting. Modern advocacy problems faced by most associations are resolved through sustained campaigns that are backed by solid strategy and well-laid plans.

A defining element of today's advocacy environment is the importance of representing the public viewpoint. The organization that can best claim to serve the public good has a far greater chance of advocacy success on any given issue. For trade groups, this can mean presenting advocacy arguments in the context of what is best for consumers. For medical groups, it can be about representing what is best for patients. Politicians respond to arguments and policy that protect the public interest. After all, the public has the final say on the future of elected leaders.

Taking the time to develop a well-thought-out advocacy approach is an important step for association leaders. The right strategy with the right planning process sets the path for lobbying victory. However, advocacy strategies do not have to be complicated. Sometimes a simple, straightforward plan trumps a time-consuming spreadsheet masterpiece.

Most importantly, advocacy plans must be flexible enough to accommodate change. They should not be fixed or rigid documents but rather living, breathing strategies that can adapt quickly to a constantly changing environment.

Much can be learned from President Eisenhower's famous line "… I have always found that plans are useless but planning is indispensable." The underlying truth is that in any campaign, be it military or political, the environment can change radically; you have to be prepared to adapt your founding strategic thinking. Factors such as media coverage, opposition tactics, elections, cabinet resignations, new information, or studies can all radically shift the advocacy environment. Association leaders must be prepared for these shifts and adapt accordingly.

Advocacy strategies can be proactive or reactive. Proactive strategies are more desirable as they are usually less costly, both in terms of dedicated financial and human resources and the mitigation of adverse effects of government regulations on members. Proactive strategies, sometimes referred to as "soft lobbying," are an attempt to put your organization ahead of the curve. However, sometimes being reactive cannot be helped—when advocacy strategies are developed in response to a particular government announcement, legislation, or impending policy.

> **The organization that can best claim to serve the public good has a far greater chance of advocacy success on any given issue.**

Chapter 2.

Developing an Advocacy Strategy

In general, highlighting issues of potential concern and providing a professional assessment of the impact on members is critical. It is important that associations continually scan the external environment and government agendas. This allows associations to be less reactive in their advocacy approach.

Guidelines for Association Advocacy

Every association should have well-established guidelines for what kinds of issues it should address and what the process is for identifying and maintaining advocacy priorities. It is critical that association leadership have a baseline for what issues should be taken on by the association.

Many times, association staff are asked to intervene on advocacy issues on an ad hoc basis by individual members. Staff must be able to asses if an issue has relevance for the overall membership or only helps a small number of members. An even more delicate scenario occurs when an association is approached to advocate on an issue that helps some members but *hinders* others. In this case, staff must be able to consult previously established guidelines for what issues are worthy of advocacy attention and which are not.

The clearer these guidelines are in advance, the faster and more responsive staff can be to member concerns. Clarity of guidelines also helps assuage members' concerns that the association is not acting on their behalf.

Each association should also have a well-established process for evaluating and prioritizing both long- and short-term government relations issues. This process can include staff evaluation of an issue against pre-set guidelines and board priorities, or it can include the work of a government relations committee or executive committee. Ultimately, the board should play a role in approving or adjusting the annual advocacy priorities.

There are several key steps involved in the advocacy planning process.

Identify and Understand the Issue

When approached with an advocacy issue, it is critical that association staff take the time to properly identify and define the issue. It is a useful practice to be able to describe the problem and its potential impact on members in one or two straightforward paragraphs. A brief written description that can be shared with and validated by key members is a worthwhile component of the planning process.

It is also important to understand the initial nuances of an issue. For example, if it is a tax matter, the association should understand which tax legislation applies and what tax interpretations have been made. Association staff should also communicate with members to understand how the tax measure is dealt with at a member level.

Developing a position is the most important component of any advocacy strategy. However, for associations with more than one member, developing a consensus around an advocacy strategy may prove daunting.

One method of soliciting membership input is through membership questionnaires. A simple questionnaire might state or review a list of key government relations issues and ask the membership to rank them in priority from most important to least important.

Once the results are tabulated, the association should have a clear direction and mandate from its members to focus on certain key issues. These questionnaires are extremely effective when conducted using the Internet.

However, time and resources do not always allow an association to canvass the entire membership for a response.

> **When approached with an advocacy issue, it is critical that association staff take the time to properly identify and define the issue.**

Chapter 2.

Developing
an Advocacy
Strategy

In my experience, using issue-specific committees is the faster and more cost-effective way to develop a position. Short-term advocacy committees, or task forces, are highly effective methods used by associations to develop positions on specific federal, provincial, or municipal issues. These committees can be highly effective in tapping member expertise and ensuring that staff fully represents member concerns.

It is impossible to have a detailed government relations or public position for every issue that might arise. Developing a position on a particular issue may take weeks or months of consultations with the membership or board. As a result, associations are left without a position when they need it most. For example, your association has an hour to respond to a journalist's deadline about an emerging public policy issue that is extremely important to your members— however, you don't have a formal position.

Build contingency plans within your organization to address these circumstances. Sometimes developing a short-term position quickly is better than having no position at all.

Set Goals

Having established a clear understanding and definition of the issue, association advocacy staff must begin the process of establishing clear lobby objectives and goals. This process can include establishing short-term objectives—for example, informing the membership of the issue. However, this process must include establishing end-goal objectives as well—that is, what victory looks like. An association starting a lobby effort must be clear which outcomes are acceptable and which alternatives are unacceptable to the membership.

It is critical at this point to consult with key members of the association, or the entire membership. Staff cannot risk defining an acceptable outcome that does not satisfy the membership. This step may seem obvious but in the practical realities of associations, it is often overlooked. The common problem is that association advocacy staff is in the middle, between government and association members. As a result, staff may have an understanding or sympathy for a government's overall policy approach that may not be clear to members or that members may not care about. Association staff must ensure they are the voice of their members to government and not the other way around.

This is not to say that helping to explain the government's rationale for a particular action or policy is not an important staff role. For example, when a government is facing a huge deficit, spending is usually curtailed; advocacy plans must take this into account. However, the members call the shots; association staff, after explaining the government's position, must ultimately represent the members.

An important element of goal-setting is to set out potential compromise positions. Given that law making and politics are built on the art of compromise, successful associations will understand that black-and-white outcomes are rarely achieved. Sometimes the price of overall lobby success is some element of compromise. Mapping out these potential positions in advance and understanding what other elements might lead to accepting a compromise are important parts of lobbying planning and strategy.

There is one important caution on compromise positions—associations must be careful not to design their own defeat. Advocacy can sometimes resemble a poker game, where revealing your cards too early can be disastrous. Telling governments or political leaders that you have a compromise position immediately puts it in play as a dominant solution. Politicians love a compromise that partially appeases different stakeholders.

> **Association staff must ensure they are the voice of their members to government and not the other way around.**

Chapter 2.

Developing an Advocacy Strategy

As a result, though it's important to consider what compromises might be acceptable, associations are usually best to hold back compromises until it is clear that it is the only way forward. Stick with your opening position until your tongue bleeds.

Research and Get the Facts

Too often associations charge off to government without the benefit of solid research or credible formal arguments, which are two foundations of successful advocacy. Credibility is key in any advocacy fight. An association that relies solely on emotional arguments or anecdotes can quickly be dismissed by government officials and politicians.

This is not to say that research and statistics alone will make your advocacy case. On the contrary, lawmakers are sometimes drowning in research and statistics. To have an impact with legislators, research must be related to real stories that bring the statistics to life. Personal association member stories help politicians understand your issue and make your overall position compelling.

Determine Your Target Audiences

A vital component of strategy is determining with whom you are trying to communicate. Are you targeting elected officials, public servants, the media, the public, or your membership? Each audience requires a slightly different approach but is built upon the same consistent advocacy message.

Understanding which group of decision makers to approach first is often one of the trickiest aspects of lobbying. At times, this may require outside professional advice.

One way for making such decisions is finding out where your issue sits in the decision-making process. For example, a particular regulation may be controlled by a senior official, with the minister's office having political oversight. Therefore, it makes sense to start with the official, and then consult the political level once you determine the state of the issue or regulation. By contrast, a parliamentary motion affecting your membership will require immediate consultations at the political level. In most cases, consulting with the motion's author and the relevant critics and committee members is a good initial approach.

Develop a Formal Position

Having a well-written formal position paper that explains your advocacy concern is important. Such a paper should include a summary of the issue, as well as key formal arguments and supporting research. The paper should also include real-life member stories that illuminate the issue and make it more personal for decision makers.

While this paper is an important basic document, it is by no means the only document you need to present your case. In most advocacy fights you need to use this core document to create other shorter, more targeted works. Key-message documents and member talking-points summarize the key points for easy review. Media statements and political summaries are also a good idea.

Detailed briefs are often more useful to government officials, as they tend to have the time and expertise to analyze them. Facts, figures, and case studies all lend credibility to your brief and if available, you should include these to illustrate your case.

Elected officials prefer executive summaries, as they are less likely to have the time to devote to a detailed brief. Summarize your key points or recommendations into no more than two pages. If it is a complex issue, the executive summary can be attached to your more formal paper.

If time constraints only allow you to produce a single brief, you must consider that it may have multiple audiences: government officials, elected officials, media, interested stakeholders, and your own members. Each group will view

Chapter 2.

Developing
an Advocacy
Strategy

your brief differently, and therefore your brief must be compiled to reach as many of these audiences as possible. Finally, avoid briefs that are overly negative or alarmist; be as constructive as possible.

If time allows, a good strategy is to provide solutions for the decision makers. Some organizations go as far as drafting actual amendments for regulations and including these in their briefs to government.

Counteract Opposition Arguments

In preparing for an advocacy campaign, associations should research the opposition to their members' advocacy case and prepare strong responses. In politics, the phrase "leave no shot unanswered" is rock-solid advice.

There are three core elements to responding to opposition positions:

1. *Acknowledge* opposition arguments

    * Accurately and dispassionately state core arguments that are used by opposing advocacy groups.

    * Do not to state these arguments weakly as "straw men" but rather lay them out impersonally and factually so they can be robustly undermined.

2. *Scrutinize* opposition arguments

    * Are their facts and research correct?

    * Are their statistics valid?

    * Is there an appeal to emotions that lacks credibility?

    * Will parliamentarians agree with their case and the core principles they appeal to?

3. *Refute* opposition arguments

    * Provide alternative research and statistics

    * Counteract emotional appeals

    * Selectively validate their concerns but point out alternative conclusions

    * Label the concerns as unfair or untrue if the label can be substantiated

Develop a Tactical Action Plan

Developing a detailed written plan that includes timelines, activities, and assignment of responsibilities is a core advocacy responsibility for association leaders. Too often, lobby efforts are unsuccessful even though the problem is identified and the objective is stated because the important tactical details needed to achieve success are absent.

This is not an argument for complex, wordy strategy documents but rather sharp, crisp, concise documents that express precisely which decision makers need to be lobbied and by whom. You must also outline what research or facts are needed for specific audiences. Research for senior official requirements can be radically different in substance than more concise political briefings.

Communicate with Your Target Audience

This is the actual process of setting up and completing meetings and outreach with the right government decision makers. Association advocates must do the legwork of establishing communications and beginning to develop relationships. In most cases, nothing beats personal one-on-one contact with decision makers. Associations cannot rely on simply sending an email or letter to the responsible minister. Instead, a formal key-contact program must be initiated. As a starting point, this might include in-person meetings with key senior officials and similar meetings with the key policy staff at the political level.

Consult Your Membership

Creating a solid feedback loop with association members on advocacy progress is fundamental to successful lobby strategy. You must continuously seek input from your membership and involve your membership in the

> Silence on the part of association staff during an advocacy campaign can too often be construed by members as inaction.

Chapter 2.

Developing an Advocacy Strategy

process. Part of this effort is simply to keep the membership informed of the association's progress on a given issue. Silence on the part of association staff during an advocacy campaign can too often be construed by members as inaction.

Frequent progress reports strengthen member support for the association and can lead to member input that helps build the overall lobby case. Consulting the membership will sometimes lead to new and important arguments and supporting facts from the field. These elements can then be used to bolster the association's advocacy case.

Consider Coalitions

Look to develop relationships with organizations of common interest. The more (credible) voices that are on your association's side, the more powerful and persuasive your lobby efforts will be. It almost goes without saying that you should avoid working with groups that lack credibility. If you unite with other groups, make sure their reputation and approach will enhance your image and not drag yours down.

Sometimes the best approach is to avoid a formal coalition in favour of more informal information sharing and coordination of tactics. This approach can be very effective by maximizing time and resource efficiency. Formal coalitions can sometimes waste time and resources because the work within the coalition can seem like action when in fact it is just background work. (See Chapter 10 for more on building coalitions.)

Review the Campaign

As a best practice, association senior staff should frequently review advocacy campaigns, and make strategic and tactical adjustments where necessary. Part of this process is seeking regular feedback from members, elected legislators, government officials, the public, and media sources.

Select a Spokesperson

An effective spokesperson must be confident, have strong public-speaking skills, be knowledgeable of the issues (both internally and externally), and appear trustworthy. Where possible, he or she should have a background in news media, or at least have media training. Bilingualism is also an asset.

A spokesperson must also be given the authority to speak on behalf of the organization and its members. He or she must have the confidence of the membership and when appropriate, speak on behalf of all members.

Some organizations use one spokesperson on all issues, while others use issue-specific spokespeople, who are more effective on highly technical issues. Remember, though, that a limited number of spokespeople ensures the message remains consistent.

Technology and Public Policy

The Internet is revolutionizing the way the public interacts with government. More and more government information is available on the Internet, and associations are putting more information online. As a result, the Internet has made communicating views and ideas between the public and government almost instantaneous.

Researching a position has never been easier. Associations are putting detailed position papers, briefs, industry facts, press releases, and even advocacy positions online, available to anyone with an Internet connection, including government policy decision makers.

Accessing services, as well as communicating with and monitoring the government, is now easier for the public to do via the Internet.

> " A spokesperson must also be given the authority to speak on behalf of the organization and its members. "

Chapter 2.

Developing an Advocacy Strategy

As a result, the policy development process is more open and allows for greater discourse with the general public. It is hoped that this transparency leads to better-developed policies.

The Internet can also be a powerful tool for associations in their efforts to lobby public policy decision makers. Used effectively, it can help you organize, mobilize, and communicate with members almost instantaneously. Brought together through shared concerns, these communities can take root and thrive due to the medium's low cost of access, unsurpassed ability to share information, and interactivity. Communities, regardless of their size, have been given a voice through this medium and can use it effectively to spread their message.

Finally, because the Internet is a relatively inexpensive communications tool to operate, this technology levels the playing field between groups varying in size and financial resources. Smaller organizations can be equally effective as larger organizations when using the Internet for advocacy purposes. Associations with limited financial resources can use the Internet to promote a viewpoint, attract supporters, and organize campaigns.

Ten Principles for Association Advocacy Success

The following elements are key principles for you to consider in building your association's advocacy approach:

1. Have an annual advocacy plan
2. Tie into the government's agenda
3. Give credit early and often
4. Be a player on every relevant government policy milestone
5. Frame advocacy in the public and consumer interest
6. Hold regular advocacy events
7. Take a multi-partisan approach

8. Understand and make use of the media

9. Seek supportive stakeholders

10. Build grassroots advocacy

PRINCIPLE ONE: Have an Annual Advocacy Plan

I cannot emphasize enough the importance of an annual advocacy plan. From my experience, this single factor can determine success or failure. I have been exposed to many unsuccessful associations that lack a lobby plan, but never an association that had a solid annual advocacy plan that did not achieve some measure of success.

While having an annual plan is a good practice and fits well with the timeline of association management and board meetings, it should not be considered a static document. As previously stated, plans must adapt frequently to changing advocacy environments.

A good annual advocacy plan prioritizes issues and resources; it also is a road map for action. It should include timelines, activities, assignments of responsibility, core arguments and research. It should also include a review of opposition resources, arguments, and counter-arguments.

PRINCIPLE TWO: Tie into the Government's Agenda

Understanding a government's overall agenda is an important initial step in moving an advocacy issue forward. Analyzing how government agenda items can support your advocacy issue and how your advocacy issue can support the government's agenda are crucial steps in your advocacy strategy.

It is easier to advance an issue that is already linked to existing government plans than to have it stand on its own.

> "While having an annual plan is a good practice and fits well with the timeline of association management and board meetings, it should not be considered a static document."

Chapter 2.

Developing an Advocacy Strategy

A simple example of this approach is arguing for a new health-care program when the government has already committed to increased health care spending. Another example is lobbying for transit funding tied into government objectives to reduce greenhouse gas emissions.

Important macro indicators of government policy intentions include:

- **Speech from the Throne**—speeches that open each parliamentary or legislature session.
- **Leaders' speeches**—where Prime Ministers, Premiers, and Mayors all lay out their plans in major public addresses.
- **Ministerial speeches**—where Cabinet ministers lay out detailed agendas in speeches and online documents.
- **Election platforms**—where political parties outline their formal positions and platforms.

Tying your issue into formal election platforms and positions can have great political value and bring an element of accountability to your issue.

Do not forget that informal intelligence gathered with political leaders can also provide insight into government plans that are yet to become public. This can be an invaluable source of information.

PRINCIPLE THREE: Give Credit Early and Often

Governments and politicians thrive on credit for decisions that help. So as advocacy success or milestones are reached, associations should give credit to those who have met with them and those who support them.

Sometimes it helps for associations to consider the politician's perspective when setting up a meeting. You should ask questions like, "What is in it for the politician?" or "What can we do to make this exchange valuable to the politician?"

At times value can come in the form of a photo opportunity

that can be used for the politician's publications or the
association's newsletters and magazines. Profiles in trade
publications also have great value for politicians and are
good venues for providing credit to political champions.

Associations should also consider creating speaking
opportunities for supportive politicians. Some associations
use podcasts or web seminars to provide championing MPs
with a broader audience. MPs can see real value in speaking
to a larger group of stakeholders via the Internet.

In my experience, it is never too early to give credit to
supporting politicians. It helps lock in their support by
demonstrating that the association is a partner in advancing
the issue and is not just a "taker." Credit in its simplest
form can be writing or emailing association members in a
given politician's riding and letting them know their elected
representative was supportive or open to dialogue.

PRINCIPLE FOUR: Be a Player on Every Relevant Government Policy Milestone

While it is never advisable to speak out without a defined
purpose, in an association advocacy context it is important
to be the voice of your members on a regular and proactive
basis. It is important that your members know you are a
serious voice on government policy milestones and that
government decision makers understand
you are a player on the larger policy
landscape. If possible, your association
should be prepared to comment on
these policy milestones and attempt to
have your issues included in major policy
indicators.

For some associations it might be an
unreasonable first step to have these
milestones address your association's
point of view. Instead, it might be better

> Sometimes it helps
> for associations to
> consider the politician's
> perspective when
> setting up a meeting.
> You should ask
> questions like,
> "What is in it for the
> politician?"

Chapter 2.

Developing an Advocacy Strategy

to seek some initial recognition of your particular issue by government. Other associations can reasonably push for their well-developed position (that has political support) to be more directly and positively addressed in a policy milestone.

Seek to have your association issue included in the following milestones:

- Speeches from the Throne
- Election platforms of all parties
- Caucus task forces
- Parliamentary committee hearings and reports
- Departmental reports
- Policy reviews and government white papers

PRINCIPLE FIVE:

Frame Advocacy in the Public and Consumer Interest

As highlighted earlier, it is fundamental for an association to be in a position to answer the question of why its "advocacy ask" is good for consumers and the general public. If an association cannot answer this question, it is starting an uphill battle. Sometimes the question of the public good has to be viewed on a timeline, meaning that an argument can be made that what is good for the consumer in the short term is not good in the long term.

Other times, the consumer argument can become the core of an association's campaign. If the public is in favour of a particular measure—and the measure provides some long-term public good—the association is no longer arguing just for its own good but also the public's. This is a great place to be in any lobby initiative.

One of my favourite examples of this is the lobbying done by transit organizations asking for increased public funding. The argument that public polls support reduced congestion and better public transit was coupled with the argument that reduced smog and emissions is good for public health.

This approach meant that the transit authorities were no longer fighting for funding for themselves; they were fighting for the public good.

PRINCIPLE SIX: Hold Regular Advocacy Events

Holding regular advocacy events to help promote your association's cause or issue is critical to building momentum and success. Events mean action and action leads to results. Examples of advocacy events with impact include:

- Annual lobby days with political leaders
- Riding awareness days, where the grassroots association members reach out to MPs when they are on a legislative break.
- Hosting key politicians at member locations—plant tours, visits to retail outlets, or hospital tours. The point is to get decision makers to feel your members' local presence.

The important thing about holding lobby events is that they require planning and contact with political leaders. All of these things provide opportunity for dialogue and advocacy advancement with political leaders.

I once encountered a Chief of Staff who arranged for his minister to meet with groups at specific planned events. This was based on the fact that the events were set in time and required planning, travel and resources. However, the same Chief of Staff frequently turned down more routine meeting requests with associations headquartered in the capital because the "minister could meet with them any time."

The reality was that "any time" became never, while the invitation to a planned event delivered the minister more often than not.

> **Association members rightly fear that playing to the opposition will alienate the elected government and make it harder to advance their cause. While this risk is real, I strongly recommend taking a multi-partisan approach when lobbying government.**

Chapter 2.

Developing an Advocacy Strategy

TIP FROM THE TRENCHES:
When Parties Change Places

I will never forget the confidential musings of a long-time opposition MP who later became a government MP and Committee Chair. He stated privately that he would never forget which associations had ignored him in opposition and now tried to deal with him as a government MP. He went on to say that those associations that dealt with him in opposition would have a "way easier time now that he was in government." This is a great example of the impact of human nature on the political process and the long-term importance of multi-partisan association lobbying.

Another important factor to consider is that not all association members support a single political party or point of view. Pandering only to the government side of a legislature risks alienating association members with different perspectives.

Lobbying opposition MPs takes on even greater importance during minority governments (more on this in Chapter 10).

PRINCIPLE SEVEN: Take a Multi-partisan Approach

One of the most frequent questions I am asked by associations is about when to approach the opposition. Association members rightly fear that playing to the opposition will alienate the elected government and make it harder to advance their cause. While this risk is real, I strongly recommend taking a multi-partisan approach when lobbying government. This is based not only on experience, but also on the need for associations to have long-term credibility no matter which party is in power.

This does not mean an association must treat all parties the same or place equal emphasis on the ruling government and the opposition. Instead, associations should allow government politicians to take the lead and take the appropriate responsibility as government members. From this point, keeping the opposition respectfully informed can help keep a lobby initiative moving forward. For strategic reasons, you do not want to provide all the details of your advocacy work with government to the opposition. However, you can touch on broad strokes and seek support. Many times I have had the experience where ministers or their staff ask an association to bring the opposition "on side," making it easier for the government to act.

As for long-term credibility, remember that today's back-bench opposition MP is tomorrow's cabinet minister; parties invariably exchange power. Recognizing that your association will have to survive such change is an important responsibility for senior staff.

PRINCIPLE EIGHT: Understand and Make Use of the Media

In many ways, media relations is a distinct discipline from government relations. However, when the media covers a public policy issue or might cover an advocacy issue, it is critical that government relations planners understand that there is a convergence of media and government relations. Although media relations in an advocacy context is covered in Chapter 8, it is important at this juncture to highlight that the media can drive a public policy issue like no other factor. Politicians and senior officials all follow the media—and to a large extent are driven by the media. Proactive use of the media to drive a government relations agenda can be highly effective on some issues. Proactively avoiding media coverage can also be an important strategy.

The key is understanding the direction media coverage is likely to take, then comprehending what impact it could have on your issue. It is an important principle to consider in

Chapter 2.

Developing an Advocacy Strategy

any advocacy endeavour. The following diagram highlights the attention paid to the media by all government decision makers. It is the one element that affects policy makers and decision makers at the same time.

> **TIP FROM THE TRENCHES: On Riding the Media Wave**
>
> "Media is the air support for the government relations ground campaign. It focuses attention and maintains momentum but it is not enough on its own. The two have to be seamlessly coordinated. Sometimes you want to create your own media wave to surf but sometimes it is more effective and less risky to surf someone else's wave. Look for opportunities to weave your story line into/onto that of existing 'hot' stories."
>
> **Andrew Casey,** Vice President, Public Affairs Forest Products Association

FIGURE 1: UNDERSTANDING GOVERNMENT
Influences on the Decision-making Process

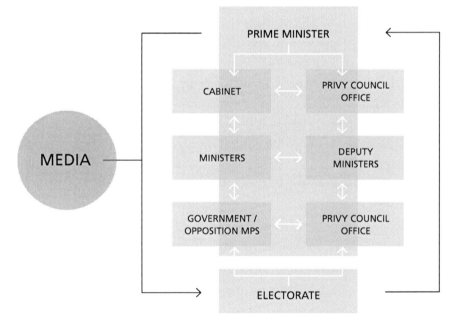

The media is the one element that affects everyone: policy makers, decision makers and the electorate.

PRINCIPLE NINE: Seek Supportive Stakeholders

Seeking a broad network of support from complementary stakeholders is a key principle of advocacy success. The best means of managing these relationships is covered in detail later in this book (see Chapter 10 for more on building coalitions) but as a starting point, lobbying strategy must consider the role of other stakeholders. As a general rule, a greater number of diverse voices, representing more voters, will produce more lobbying impact. Conversely, associating with a discredited group, or a group that is at odds with government, can sink a campaign. Choosing the right partners with complementary messages is critical to success.

PRINCIPLE TEN: Build Grassroots Advocacy

In my experience, the most overlooked aspect of lobbying strategy by Canadian association executives is the use of grassroots lobbying. Too often, executives view this as too hard to generate, or as something the association should do for its members, rather than ask its members to do. This kind of thinking is easy if you have not experienced the power of grassroots campaigns. The power comes in two forms.

First, it achieves astonishing results that staff cannot achieve on their own. Second, it builds a great long-term relationship between the association and its members. The little-known adage, "if you want a friend, ask someone to do you a favour," is very powerful. Once someone does you a favour, he or she has an investment in your success. It works like that in politics and with grassroots lobbying.

On countless occasions, I have had association executives rave about the role of grassroots activity when properly rolled out. For more on how to do this, see Chapter 9.

> In my experience, the most overlooked aspect of lobbying strategy by Canadian association executives is the use of grassroots lobbying.

Federal and Provincial Governments

Chapter 3.

Federal and Provincial Governments

Understanding Government Departments

"Bureaucracy" and "bureaucrats" are common names given to government departments and those who work in them. While these terms might be acceptable to the average person, individuals employed in government consider them pejorative. The terms tend to carry the negative connotation of "paper pusher" so it is best to avoid them.

The public service consists of government officials that are employed by various government departments. These officials administer the government—the daily operations of governing. More importantly, however, government officials provide advice to successive governments on policy. It is this expert advice that ministers rely on to develop regulations, policies, and laws.

Line departments, such as Transport Canada, Environment Canada, or Human Resources and Skills Development Canada, administer government programs or services at the federal level. In provincial jurisdictions, line departments include departments responsible for such areas as tourism, education, or social services. These departments are also the incubators of government policy.

At both levels of government, central agencies—for example, Department of Finance, Treasury Board Secretariat, or the Privy Council Office—oversee all departments or coordinate their functioning from a specific point of view.

By necessity, line departments often compete with each another for limited financial resources to fund programs and services.

Public servants from line departments are often the most important influencing point of any advocacy issue. They are the front line of government policy development and research, and ultimately of legislation and regulations. These line department officials also play a central role in the allocation of program funding and the administration of key programs. As such, line department officials are primary contacts for associations wanting to change government decisions and for ongoing policy development. Too often, association advocacy efforts overlook the power and influence of front-line public servants like these.

Ongoing Government Monitoring

Successful government relations is about being ahead of the curve. Be aware of developments and stay informed. As well as allowing your organization an opportunity to participate in the process, this knowledge demonstrates your organization's value to its membership. This achievement, however, requires constant monitoring of government.

The most effective government monitoring involves a substantial commitment of time and resources. However, there are some simple actions you can take to stay informed of government announcements.

Email

Many government departments make announcements available to the public by email. By visiting the government department's website, you can register an email account and receive press releases, speeches, and announcements directly by email.

Mailing Lists

Register your organization on as many government or stakeholder mailing lists as possible. Contact government

> **Line department officials are primary contacts for associations wanting to change government decisions and for ongoing policy development.**

Chapter 3.

Federal and Provincial Governments

officials, elected representatives, political party organizations, or other associations with similar interests and request that your organization be added to their mailing lists.

While mailing lists and emails will keep you informed, they alone will not keep you ahead of the curve. Your goal is to be aware of issues and leading the process long before the government issues a public announcement.

Federal and Provincial Elected Officials

Keeping government officials informed of industry trends, issues, events, discussion groups, or research is an important part of any government relations strategy. You need to put officials on your mailing lists, or prepare special government bulletins, newsletters, or news releases.

Some associations grant government departments associate membership status, while other associations may be successful in signing up government departments as full members.

The goal is to create an ongoing dialogue between your organization and officials by involving officials when designing surveys, polls, or research questions. If strategically prudent, you can even give officials advance notice of an upcoming advocacy campaign, or ask officials to provide your organization with input and advice on issues.

Find, create, or invent opportunities to communicate frequently with government officials responsible for areas of interest to your organization or membership.

However, one of the challenges many associations face is determining which politicians are important to a given issue. Analyzing which elected officials are main committees members, Committee Chairs, on Caucus committees, or in cabinet roles is necessary, but takes time.

In addition, it is critical to highlight which politicians are most interested in a given issue. Reviewing voting records, past careers, community positions, and a politician's pattern of legislative and policy work may help determine this.

It is equally important to define closely which government officials are important to an advocacy campaign. In most cases, several layers of government officials are involved in major decisions. It is important to understand reporting structures within departments and not to ignore the important influence of lower-level officials.

Elected Officials and Their Staff

Elected officials at the provincial and federal levels fill many roles—not only as representatives of their constituents and loyal party members, but also as ombudsmen and lawmakers attempting to hold the government accountable.

On a typical day, an elected official might: meet with the media, members of the public, or colleagues; respond to a mountain of correspondence and telephone messages; prepare speeches; and review background documents for their committee work. It is a job that takes them on a well-worn path between parliamentary and constituency offices, caucus or committee rooms, and between public events. For most elected officials, it involves long hours.

To assist in his or her duties, the parliamentarian hires staff in both the legislative and constituency offices. It is important to understand that not every minister's office has the same organizational structure. Different structures may depend on departmental priorities or on a minister's unique personal management style.

Political staff can also have different latitude for decision making depending on the minister's trust and even the

> " While mailing lists and emails will keep you informed, they alone will not keep you ahead of the curve. Your goal is to be aware of issues and lead the process long before the government issues a public announcement. "

Chapter 3.

**Federal and
Provincial
Governments**

relationship with the department. A strict organizational chart never tells the whole story to associations dealing with a minister's office. Given these factors, it is still important to understand the general roles and responsibilities of an elected official's staff.

Chief of Staff

The chief of staff reports directly to the minister, and he or she usually has overall responsibility for advising on legislative proposals, political decisions, and constituency matters. The chief of staff is the person in charge of overall office operations, including assigning work and managing staff. The chief of staff also plays a key role as a liaison with the most senior departmental officials in the minister's portfolio. The chief of staff can also take the role of senior negotiator with stakeholder groups prior to ministerial meetings or ministerial decisions.

Deputy Chief of Staff

This is a new role primarily at the federal level to relieve the administration and policy burden on chiefs of staff.

Director of Policy

Generally speaking, this role is reserved for individuals with a background in research and policy development. These individuals tend to work closely with department officials in examining the policy implications of political files. They can be an important resource to help associations understand both the political and departmental perspective on an issue.

Policy Advisor

This is a role similar to the director of policy but generally manages fewer issues and does not have an overall policy oversight responsibility.

Director of Parliamentary Affairs

This role is primarily in large minister's offices and encompasses working with the minister's caucus colleagues, parliamentary committees, and the legislative process. This role can be a key resource on issues that are actively under debate in the legislature.

Legislative Assistant

The legislative assistant (LA) is usually the staff person who monitors legislation and policy issues, and advises on daily government procedures. In opposition offices, the LA develops questions for Question Period, while in ministerial offices the LA briefs and prepares ministers for possible questions. In smaller offices, the executive assistant (see below) is also the legislative assistant.

Director of Communications

This role is generally responsible for all aspects of ministerial communications, including media-related communications and communications items for the public and stakeholders. In larger ministerial offices, this individual works closely with the press secretary, who handles the more direct contact with the media. In smaller ministerial offices, the director of communications performs both duties.

Press Secretary

The press secretary is responsible for interacting with the media; advising, developing, and delivering the official message; and acting as the official spokesperson of the elected official. Only offices with added responsibility and larger budgets employ press secretaries, such as ministerial offices or the opposition leader's office. In smaller offices, the executive or legislative assistant doubles as the press secretary.

Special Assistants

Special assistants often handle the parliamentarian's general day-to-day duties, including scheduling, correspondence, and some constituency casework. In larger offices,

> **The chief of staff can also take the role of senior negotiator with stakeholder groups prior to ministerial meetings or ministerial decisions.**

Chapter 3.

Federal and Provincial Governments

these assistants might be assigned a specific responsibility such as a policy file, issue, or regional area.

Scheduling Assistant

The scheduling assistant is responsible for allocating the parliamentarian's time among the many demands that arise. He or she may also be responsible for making travel arrangements, arranging speaking dates and appearances, and coordinating activities in the parliamentarian's constituency office. The scheduling assistant often doubles as the Special Assistant mentioned above.

Executive Assistant

At the provincial level, executive assistants often play the role of chief of staff, in that they have overall responsibility for advising on legislative proposals, political decisions, and constituency matters. They are also in charge of overall office operations. The title can be misleading to those outside government who may assume this is more of a secretarial role. At the federal level, this role is often aimed at making the minister more efficient in his or her role.

Constituency Assistant

Constituency assistants are the staff members usually assigned to resolve specific constituent-related matters (examples of federal issues include passports, immigration or social benefits). Constituency assistants also schedule the parliamentarian's time while in the constituency.

Meeting with Public Servants

Meeting and working with government officials is one of the most important components of a government relations strategy; however, it is the most under-utilized approach by associations.

As mentioned earlier, officials are not only administrators of programs and services; they are also drafters of policy and legislation. Contrary to popular belief, government officials often seek outside advice and are willing to consult with organizations prior to developing policies and regulations that affect your members or constituency.

Therefore, associations can be a welcome resource to government. Your organization has access to real-world experiences, data, or members willing to provide practical evidence to government officials planning policy or regulations. Associations are easier for government officials to consult—one voice representing an entire community—than hundreds of individual members.

Government officials also look to associations to assist in communicating government messages to their members. An association's internal communications methods and programs are of real interest to government officials. A good government relations strategy seeks opportunities to meet or communicate with government officials with responsibility for issues of mutual interest on a regular basis.

> **Associations are easier for government officials to consult— one voice representing an entire community— than hundreds of individual members.**

Chapter 4.

Meeting with Public Servants

The Elevator Pitch

Being able to explain who your association is, and what your advocacy concerns are, in a short concise statement is an invaluable advocacy tool. This presentation should not appear rehearsed but instead be a conversational expression of who the association represents and what it stands for.

Often this approach is labelled the elevator pitch because around Parliament Hill or other government offices, association advocates often meet elected officials in the elevator, hallways, or entrances. The officials will often introduce themselves; an elevator pitch is the perfect way to take advantage of an impromptu—and brief—meeting with a decision maker. A well-honed elevator pitch also comes in handy during political fundraising events or receptions where elected officials must work the room and only have a short time with each guest. Such pitches can also be useful for airplane conversations or at baggage claim. The point is that association leaders should always be ready to brand their association in a leader's mind and hit one core concern.

As mentioned, a good elevator pitch cannot seem to be too rehearsed or robotic. This doesn't mean that rehearsal is not required; it just means that you have to practise a relaxed, informal delivery. A good pitch highlights who you are and what your association represents.

If you represent medical laboratory technicians, you can use a meaningful or colourful example: "My association represents medical laboratory technicians. We are the lab-coat folks on whose work 85 per cent of doctors' decisions are made." If you represent librarians, you can say something like, "We are the association that represents more libraries in Canada than there are Tim Hortons!"

If time and context allow, the pitch should move gracefully to highlight your one key concern. For example, "We are on the Hill to talk about better funding for medical labs."

Or, "We are concerned about the government postal funding for library users."

The important goal of the pitch is to create a brand or an image for the decision makers. Too often, it is assumed that officials understand association names and acronyms. The reality is that elected officials are so swamped with issues that they need help understanding context and the meaning of different groups.

As an example, the average official may understand what insurance is but not understand that there is a big distinction between insurance companies and local insurance brokers. Similarly, there is a big difference between property insurance and life insurance. In another example, officials might not understand the difference between car manufacturers and parts makers or even locally owned dealerships. Never assume an official will understand your industry; instead paint a mental picture that will stick. For example, "I represent the over 3,000 locally-owned car dealerships of different manufacturers from Ford to Toyota."

To turn this into an even more memorable phrase it should include a reference to the official's own riding. For example, "I represent the over 3,000 locally-owned car dealerships of different manufacturers from Ford to Toyota. We have ten dealerships in your riding and John Smith Ford in your riding is a member of our Board." That paints a picture!

With the library sector, it might be, "I represent the library community and we have more libraries in Canada than there are Tim Hortons; in your riding, Smith University is a large member of ours."

A local tie-in busts through the clutter of everyday responsibilities and demonstrates why an elected official should care. If time or circumstance allow, you should also highlight your key concern and explain why the official should support your association. You might choose

Chapter 4.

Meeting
with Public
Servants

to mention a positive meeting with his or her political colleague or party leadership, or tie into a specific local concern.

If you get the chance, tell the official briefly what action you would request of them or suggest a future meeting to discuss the sector.

The most important thing to be careful of in an elevator pitch is never to press too hard or oversell the opportunity. If the official is talking on the phone or engaged with a staffer on an important conversation, do not butt in. The normal rules of polite conduct apply. Some officials bristle at being interrupted. There is, however, a need to be opportunistic—but not rude—and sometimes that is a fine line. Even after the conversation is underway, you must be careful about overextending your time and advocacy approach.

Practise your elevator pitch with other staff members and even engage the board in developing the key components of an elevator pitch. Shaping a message about who you are and what you want in less than 30 seconds can be a great exercise for sharpening priorities. Making sure that board members can deliver the elevator pitch can also be valuable. They frequently are the best cheerleaders of the association among other members and frequently have opportunities with local leaders. The more these association leaders can deliver a quick concise explanation of who they are and what they want, the better off the association will be.

A useful exercise I sometime conduct with association boards and staff is: "Thirty Seconds with the Mayor, Premier, MP or Prime Minister." It can be a welcome break to routine board meetings and it will arm your association leaders with some real advocacy skills that will help the association. Such exercises also make board members keenly aware of the challenge of delivering a lobby message under tight timelines.

TIP FROM THE TRENCHES: Don't Force It

One of my favourite examples was the rare opportunity
I had to be seated on a short flight next to a federal
leader whom I did not know at the time. Rather
than press an introduction at the beginning of the
flight and risk looking like a pushy lobbyist, I instead
chose to hold back and treat him like any other
anonymous business traveler—in other words, polite
indifference. This was not easy to do because there
was so much I wanted to convey to the leader about
the association and our advocacy agenda. Well, as
the saying goes, "all good things come to those who
wait." After nearly 40 minutes of the hour-long
flight, the politician broke first, introduced himself
and enquired about me. After some brief opening
conversation, I worked in the association elevator
pitch and was met with a sustained and interested
line of questions about our core issues and political
concerns. It was a beautiful 20 minutes of advocacy
that never seemed like lobbying—just two passengers
exchanging views. I am sure that if I had pressed the
attack in the opening minutes of the flight, there
would have been much less open dialogue. In the end,
I was able to deliver key messages and build a lasting
relationship for both the association and the politician.

Requesting a Meeting

As mentioned earlier, a scheduling assistant is responsible
for managing the elected official's time. This person
coordinates all meeting requests as well as other scheduling
demands such as house duty, committee schedules, travel,
and personal obligations. When requesting a meeting with
an official, the scheduling assistant is usually the first or last
staff member you speak to before a meeting takes place.

Chapter 4.

Meeting with Public Servants

TIP FROM THE TRENCHES: Don't Discount Staff

Too often, senior members of the private sector or an association mistakenly assume that people in their twenties or early thirties are junior office staff of little political importance. This can be a serious mistake and lead to some major blunders. I have a vivid memory of an association staff member barking at a young staffer to make sure there was water for her members' meeting with the Prime Minister, only to discover later that the young staffer was the Prime Minister's chief of staff. Not exactly good relationship-building and government relations.

On another occasion I witnessed an association member on a grassroots lobby day treat an office assistant rudely. The association member had no idea that this particular staff member made all of the MP's scheduling and time allocation decisions. Only some well-timed flowers and an appropriate apology ensured future advocacy.

It is critical to be polite and considerate of all staff. As a rule, staff members in political offices are younger than in the private sector and carry more responsibility than their age might convey.

Scheduling assistants need to know the purpose of the meeting, who is attending, a brief description of your organization, your preferred date, time, and location, and the anticipated length of the meeting. Providing this information in writing increases your likelihood of success.

The scheduling assistant then meets with the chief of staff or the official directly to discuss all requests. Depending on the official's availability, interest in an issue, or priorities, your request is either granted or denied. The scheduling assistant will inform you of the outcome of your request.

Prior to the Meeting

If you are bringing a delegation, keep it to three people or fewer. Provide the office with names, titles, addresses, and biographies of the delegates. To ensure the meeting is most effective, provide a background note that includes the issue or concern, any recommendations your organization is proposing, information on the industry, or a list of your members in their constituency.

This information helps the elected official prepare for the meeting. Remember to keep the information concise and contained within two pages. Anything longer and you risk losing your audience.

During the Meeting

Keep in mind that most elected officials have very busy agendas; therefore, you should be brief and to the point. Try to keep the meeting short, between 15 and 30 minutes. Before meeting the official, the delegation should decide on a principal spokesperson to handle the main points. All members of the delegation should feel free to comment at any time, however.

Open the meeting by thanking the official for having taken the time from his or her busy schedule to meet with you and your colleagues. Introduce yourself as well as the other members of your delegation by giving your name, title, company, as well as its location.

Say a few words about the purpose and aim of your meeting. Sample reasons for your meeting might include:

- Promoting a better understanding and appreciation among parliamentarians of a particular industry

> **It is critical to be polite and considerate of all staff. As a rule, staff members in political offices are younger than in the private sector and carry more responsibility than their age might convey.**

- Building a long-lasting relationship with the parliamentarian
- Urging the official to support a particular policy
- Educating the official on the benefits of a policy to his or her community.

Chapter 4.

Meeting with Public Servants

TIP FROM THE TRENCHES: Don't Talk Too Much

While most people outside the lobbying profession think that slick talking is the most powerful skill of a lobbyist, nothing is further from the truth. Lobbying is best accomplished by listening to decision makers, learning their point of view, and understanding potential objections. Then, it is the art of subtly addressing their concerns and overcoming their objections. Early in my career, I watched in great pain as a senior association executive tried to bluster past an experienced MP with a set line of debate, without ever hearing the MP's point of view or pausing to hear questions or concerns. It was a disaster only saved by the MP, who took charge of the situation and pointed out that his concerns needed to be heard.

Everybody likes to be heard, especially if they are elected to represent the people.

If applicable, stress the importance of your concern to the elected official's region and how the industry serves the needs of his or her constituents. Also note, where applicable, that you will be reporting on your meeting to people in the industry and their employees in his or her constituency.

At the close of your meeting, briefly summarize the key points on the issue(s) you are raising. Leave a one- or two-page synopsis of your industry or concern, or a brochure. Do not inundate the official with briefing material, as he or she will then be more likely to file the information or pass it off to a staff member to summarize.

Remember, you want to develop a long-term relationship with this public policy decision maker. Anything you can do to be a continuing resource of facts and statistics, or simply a barometer of your industry, will go a long way toward a more positive outcome.

Build in some "about you" time. Ask elected officials if your organization can be of any assistance to them. Listen to pet projects that they might be involved with. If you are unable to assist, at least you will be able to raise the issue as a point of interest next time you meet with the official. These steps help build the relationship.

Before leaving your meeting, thank the official for the opportunity to talk about your concern or industry. If you haven't already done so, present your business card and urge the official to contact you for more information.

Most parliamentarians will add your name to their mailing lists and you will receive newsletters, flyers, and invitations to special events including fundraising receptions. These mailings will keep you informed and provide you with an opportunity to be more engaged in the public policy decision-making process.

Making Elected Officials Aware of Your Association's Local Impact

One of the stark realities of political life is that elected officials are generally forced to be more concerned with the local impact of an issue than with the details of a policy brief. Sometimes the most important part of your association's advocacy case is geography.

Tying your association's overall advocacy request to key local elements is critical. If you have members in an elected official's riding, highlight them. If your members have suppliers, customers, or stakeholders in the politician's riding, underscore it. If your association has no link to the riding, highlight similar ties to the province or region.

Chapter 4.

Meeting
with Public
Servants

As you make your case, lawmakers will be far more receptive to local research and statistics than national ones. Real-life stories from their riding are excellent attention-getters and will have more impact than general statements. Meeting with an elected official also provides an invaluable potential for linking members in that riding with the official. This is where central association meetings with politicians can dovetail nicely with grassroots lobby efforts. Elected officials want to connect with local stakeholders, and association meetings can help facilitate this. You should be proactive and ask if the official is open to future meetings with local members or local tours that involve members' facilities.

While I would never suggest building an advocacy case without facts, there is definitely a place for well-placed emotional arguments when laying out the case before a politician. For example, if you are making the case for better funding for cancer research, personal examples of friends, family, and community members will resonate more than statistics. Likewise, pleading the case for a small-business issue is better done by giving personal examples of the business's community impact or local employees affected.

After the Meeting

Send a letter thanking the official for meeting with you. Briefly reiterate the issue, or address any points raised in the meeting. Keep notes or a database of the people you meet with. I recommend that you develop a de-briefing questionnaire that allows you to track positions, points of interest, or facts. These questionnaires help your organization follow up with any obligations or clarify a particular statement. More importantly, it allows your organization to pass this organizational memory on to other members or personnel that might meet with the same individual in the future.

Building and Maintaining Relationships

Too often, directors of not-for-profit organizations visit elected officials only when there is a problem or when they need a solution. Strong relationships with elected officials, however, are developed, maintained, and nourished when there is no immediate concern or issue. In short, visit elected officials in good times, as well as bad.

Hold friendly meet-and-greets. Simply update officials on your activities or offer assistance with issues or projects of interest to them. If applicable, assist them in resolving constituency matters. Be a resource to elected officials and lend your organization's assistance to their offices.

Seek or create opportunities to promote the official within your membership or with members located in the politician's electoral district. Invite them to attend or deliver speeches at product launches, openings, board meetings, annual conferences, and conventions. Photo-ops with officials can be used for internal publications, trade magazines, or mainstream media distribution. They might use your photos in their own newsletters or mailings to their constituents.

Personally attend or encourage members to attend political events including fundraisers, town hall meetings, announcements, or social events such as barbecues, holiday parties, or levies.

Also, encourage members to become active in campaigns, purchase party memberships, or participate on riding association executive committees.

Anything your organization can do to develop long-term relationships with elected officials will go a long way to assisting your government relations efforts.

> " While I would never suggest building an advocacy case without facts, there is definitely a place for well-placed emotional arguments when laying out the case before a politician. "

Appearing Before Legislative Committees

Chapter 5.

Appearing Before Legislative Committees

The bulk of officials' parliamentary work is done in committee. There, they study issues, examine legislation and review departmental spending plans (known as Estimates). Members of a legislative committee are expected to read background documents and meet experts in the field, including lawyers, economists, special interest groups, business people, and senior government officials.

At the federal level, MPs are assigned at least two committees on average. There are about 20 permanent or "standing" committees. There are also special committees set up to consider a specific issue or bill. Committees can sit from 6 to 40 hours per week and many travel across the country to hear witnesses. Working on committees enables MPs to study issues and legislation in greater detail than is possible in the Chamber.

The Senate has a similar committee structure. A significant difference between Senate and House committees, however, is that while Senators are partisan, they are appointed, not elected. Therefore, Senate committees have a certain level of independence and have been known to contradict, amend, and even initiate government policy. Senators and Senate committees can be extremely useful in your advocacy efforts.

In most cases, appearing before a committee is beneficial to the organization. The organization can promote itself among key public-policy decision makers, advance its concerns, and be seen by the membership as providing a members' service. However, sometimes it is more beneficial to the organization *not* to appear before a committee.

Depending on the issue, circumstances, or political climate, avoiding committees or "keeping one's head down" might be more advantageous. This is a decision that the organization must assess when considering appearing before a committee.

Getting an Invitation to Appear

Witnesses are guests of committees and appear at the invitation of the committee. There is no guarantee that your organization will be invited to appear before a parliamentary committee, even during public consultations.

The process of scheduling witnesses varies among committees, depending on the authority the committee members have vested in the Clerk. Some committees instruct the Clerk to schedule witnesses automatically, especially during large or regular sessions such as the annual pre-budget consultations. Other committees review the witness list and choose their witnesses based on considerations varying from relevance of subject matter to time constraints to political manoeuvrings. Steering committees, usually comprising one committee member from each political party, are responsible for setting the committee agenda and selecting witnesses, except where that responsibility is delegated to the Clerk.

If your organization decides that it wants to appear before a committee, here are steps you may take to increase this likelihood of being invited:

- Write to the Clerk of the Committee requesting an opportunity to appear on a given subject. Provide a short description of the organization, its mandate, and membership base. Include names and titles of witnesses. Provide a contact address, telephone and fax numbers, and email address. Also include a preferred location if the committee is holding regional or cross-country consultations. Preferred dates or requests to appear

Chapter 5.

Appearing Before Legislative Committees

together with particular witnesses are accommodated when feasible.

- Write a similar letter to the committee chair and all members of the committee, with your request to appear.

- Speak to the committee chair regarding your request. Also, speak to members of the Steering Committee. Don't hesitate to utilize your membership. If a member of your organization lives with, works with, or knows a committee member personally, have that person contact the elected official on behalf of the organization. The Clerk of the Committee can provide you with names and contact numbers of committee members.

- Find some direct benefit for the committee members to hear from your organization. If the witness is from a region or constituency relevant to a committee member, inform the elected official of this fact.

Delivering a Memorable Presentation

- Bring a photographer and take pictures prior to the start of the hearing of your witnesses engaged in discussion with committee members (first seek permission from the Clerk of the Committee) and provide copies of these photos to committee members for use in their publications.

- Keep your presentation short. Give committee members the "gift of time."

- Don't be afraid to engage in debate. However, if you don't have the answer, don't make it up. Let the committee know that you would be pleased to follow up with a reply to that specific question.

- Be an expert on your issue or a resource to the membership.

For more information, we have a handy checklist:

CHECKLIST:
Appearing Before Parliamentary Committees

☐ *Arrive 15 to 30 minutes prior to your scheduled presentation.* This allows you time to register with the Clerk of the Committee, acquaint yourself with members of the committee, and settle in.

☐ *Pick a seat in the middle of the witness table.* If the Clerk has not assigned seating to you, feel free to sit in the witness section (usually opposite the Clerk).

☐ *Pour yourself a glass of water.* Water containers and glasses should be provided for you on the witness table. Pour yourself a glass of water. Do not pour water while speaking or once the committee hearings have begun, as this can be a distraction. (Beware of the overflowing ice.)

☐ *Hook up to translation devices.* Committee hearings are conducted in both official languages, and simultaneous translation is provided. Connect to the translation devices and take a moment to tune into the channel that you need. If committee members ask you a question, you may reply in either official language.

☐ *Check your notes and review your speech.* Take a moment to ensure that you have all your documents organized and laid out in front of you. Review your speech quickly.

☐ *Don't play with the microphone.* In front of you there will be a microphone. When speaking, ensure that the microphone is pointed toward you. An operator in the room will activate the microphone from a central console and a red light will appear on the base of the microphone when it is live. There is no need to press the button at the base.

Chapter 5.

Appearing Before Legislative Committees

During the Hearing

After all committee members have taken their seats, the committee chair will call the meeting to order. He or she will state the purpose of the hearing and welcome witnesses. The chair will provide witnesses with instructions, set the time limit for opening remarks, and call on the first witness on the witness list. The witness usually has three to five minutes to make opening remarks.

Once the witness has concluded opening remarks, the chair will thank that witness and then call the next witness. This process continues until all the witnesses have presented their opening remarks.

The chair will then turn the floor over to the committee members for questions. The first question is usually allotted to the Official Opposition. The question may be directed at any particular witness or to all witnesses. Answer the question to the best of your knowledge.

After the question and answer component of the hearing is concluded, the chair will instruct the witnesses to provide the committee with a one-minute summary of their presentation. This is an opportunity for you to state in point form the key points of your presentation or to call on the committee for a particular action.

The chair will then thank the witnesses for their presentations and conclude the hearing.

TIP FROM THE TRENCHES: Handling Q & A

Remember that you are dealing with politicians. Questions may not always be questions but rather opportunities for them to grandstand on an issue. Be patient and listen carefully. Furthermore, sometimes the tone of the question may make the questioner appear adversarial when in actuality he or she is a supporter. Take the time necessary to think about your response and don't be afraid to keep it short.

Finally, the committee is an extension of the chamber so procedural rules that govern the chamber apply to the committee. Sometimes, but not often, procedural debates or political battles may occur between committee members during the hearings. Should this take place, be patient and wait for instructions from the Chair. Do not become involved, take a side, or comment, even if asked to.

After the Hearing

Dealing with Committee Members

Committee members may approach you to thank you for your presentation or to clarify a point that you made. Also, feel free to approach committee members to thank them for their support, especially if you know the member or the member is the local politician in your area.

Dealing with the Media

If the hearing is open to the public, the media is permitted to view the proceedings. Make yourself available to the media by staying a few minutes after the conclusion of the hearing. If you speak to journalists, ask them what media outlet they represent. This will enable you to track down the story the next day.

Ministers and Their Offices

Chapter 6.

Ministers and Their Offices

In the Canadian parliamentary system the vast majority of political power—the ability to move the machinery of government—resides with ministers of the Crown and their offices. Cabinet ministers are the ultimate decision makers for the government departments they oversee. In addition, cabinet ministers play a key role in shaping all major government initiatives when they sit together as a group and review policy at weekly cabinet meetings. Developing and maintaining good relationships with these ministers and their staff is therefore crucial to the success of any association with a significant lobby agenda.

Building and Maintaining Relationships

The snapshot of political staff and politicians as extremely busy individuals pulled in many different directions by competing interests is a reality at all levels of government in Canada. The fact of life for cabinet ministers and their aides is that these demands are extreme and can at times reach a fevered pitch.

Canadian cabinet ministers are elected and owe much of their success to political supporters. As a result, there has always been a need for ministers to employ politically minded individuals to aid them in helping shape government policy. These political staffers, or aides, are not permanent members of the public service but are hired by ministers to act as advisors, liaisons, and administrators.

Since the 1980s, political staff has grown both in number and in influence on the actions of government. In some cases, ministerial staff can play a more significant role shaping government policy than senior officials. In other more traditional cases, ministers' staffs simply provides an extra set of eyes and ears for the minister and play a role of assisting communication between the minister and outside interests groups. As a general rule, the minister sets the parameters for the role of political staff, with some ministers granting wide latitude and others keeping their staff under far tighter control.

In either case, it is important for associations to understand that ministers divide their department's areas of responsibility among their political staff. Generally speaking, these divisions mirror the shape of the department's basic structure, but not always. Political assistants are then responsible for keeping the minister informed on these areas and for meeting with external interest groups related to their files or "desk."

Meeting with Ministers' Staff

Because of the pivotal role ministers' staff plays in the political process, it is important to maintain good relationships with those staffers responsible for your area of interest in ministers' offices.

The challenge for associations is to strike a delicate balance between keeping in touch with minister's offices and wearing out their welcome. This balance is not easy but successful associations find a way to be considerate of the time demands in a minister's office; unsuccessful associations get lost in their own self-importance and quickly alienate key players.

An informal meeting over coffee or a short telephone discussion can be as valuable as more formal meetings. These quick hits allow associations to stay in touch with ministers and their teams without taking

> **The challenge for associations is to strike a delicate balance between keeping in touch with minister's offices and wearing out their welcome.**

valuable time. The key to getting your phone calls returned by busy ministers' offices is always to offer value. Is there some new piece of information or an update on an event that is useful for the political staff to know or understand?

The Commodity of Politics Is Information

Chapter 6.

Ministers and Their Offices

Wise politicians have long talked about the concept of information as the elixir of politics. In Ottawa, information is often seen as a commodity to be traded. This is as true on Parliament Hill among MPs and Senators as it is among officials in various departments. Information is central to politics and to shaping the policy process. Associations active in government relations live on the edge of the political life in the nation's capital. A good government relations staffer will drift in and out of official Ottawa gathering information and, almost as importantly, passing on information. To be successful in the long term, an association lobbyist should become an unofficial part of the Ottawa establishment, dispensing and accepting information of value.

> ### TIP FROM THE TRENCHES: Cut Through the Clutter
>
> "MPs and their staffers are extremely over-loaded with information and solicitations from various interest groups. I have found that if you want to cut through the clutter you must keep your message short, compelling and easy to understand. In other words, get to the point and show that you can solve his or her problem."
>
> **Bruce R. Burrows** Vice President, Public and Corporate Affairs, The Railway Association of Canada

Meeting with Ministers

A meeting with a cabinet minister can be a very important part of the political process but it is not always necessary. Indeed, the vast majority of association lobby problems are solved well below the level of the minister.

Many associations have wasted valuable time and effort during lobby campaigns by targeting ministers unnecessarily.

Because there is no hard and fast rule for determining the involvement of ministers, it is important for associations to investigate this question on an individual basis before seeking to involve the minister. As a guideline, however, it is possible to say that the bigger and more far-reaching a policy decision is, the more likely it is that a given minister will need to provide his or her final approval.

It should also be pointed out that ministers can play a substantial role in overruling or altering the direction of their department. In this way, ministers act as a court of last resort if association lobby efforts fail at the lower levels of bureaucracy. Associations may approach a minister to review decisions or policy directives already established by department officials. Associations need to proceed with great caution in this area, as there is a real risk of alienating officials if these requests are not handled professionally.

It is also important to note that, in most cases, associations should involve their most senior elected members or industry representatives in a meeting with the minister. While the senior association staff might attend the meeting, ministers expect to hear directly from association leaders.

In general, the principles of meeting with elected officials apply to meeting with ministers. However, remember that a minister will likely bring senior officials to the meeting to serve as a resource and to provide follow-up action.

Given the increased importance of ministers, it is crucial to add an enhanced level of preparation to pre-meeting efforts. Know your minister. Research past speeches, positions, statements and articles,

> "The bigger and more far-reaching a policy decision is, the more likely it is that a given minister will need to provide his or her final approval."

or any other information that provide an insight into the individual. Understand the minister's relationship with his or her department and deputy minister. Is it adversarial or collegial? Weak or strong? Master and servant? If so, who is the master—the minister or the department?

Chapter 6.

Ministers and Their Offices

Meeting with Prime Ministers and Premiers

Never underestimate your ability to raise your issues to the highest level. Ultimately, the buck stops with the Prime Minister or Premier. While it takes more effort to bring your issue directly to the head of government, don't be reluctant to pursue this course of action, especially if you believe other avenues may be less successful. The head of government is an elected official like all others, and the methods used to build relationships with the head of government remain the same.

Using your membership in his or her constituency remains effective. Whether Prime Minister or Premier, they are still elected members of parliament or the legislature and need to maintain relationships with the electoral district they represent.

CHECKLIST: Meeting Elected Officials

☐ *Has the association carefully selected spokespeople? Are they individuals that the minister will easily relate to? Have regional, language, and other background factors been taken into consideration?*

☐ *Given the limited meeting time, have the spokespeople rehearsed key messages and practised responses to likely questions?*

☐ *Does the association have something new to offer during the meeting? Member surveys, polling, or other new research can be put to valuable use with ministers.*

☐ *Have association staff members held detailed conversations with ministerial staff to shape the parameters of the meeting and help anticipate areas of discussion?*

☐ *Have you alerted the minister's office as to names, titles, addresses and biographies of delegates?*

☐ *Will any aides or officials accompany the minister? If yes, who are they and what are their responsibilities?*

☐ *Should you send briefing material and "leave-behinds" in advance? Sometimes, to avoid interference from unfriendly officials that might block or pre-judge your arguments, it is advisable not to send this material in advance.*

TIP FROM THE TRENCHES: Say Thank You

Sometimes the most important meeting with a minister is held for the purpose of saying thank you. Too often, associations fight a hard lobby campaign and forget to give credit to the appropriate minister. This can be a fatal blow to an association's long-term credibility. A formal meeting to say thank you and an accompanying photo and article in the association's publications can go a long way to establishing future positive relations with a given minister.

From No Federal Funds to Over $5 Billion in 10 years

CASE STUDY

A decade ago, the Canadian Urban Transit Association (CUTA) felt it was spinning its wheels. Transit was off the federal government's priority list and federal funding was at zero.

CUTA, dedicated to being the voice of urban transit in Canada, had the ultimate advocacy campaign goal to have public transit properly recognized by the government and to have funding increased.

CUTA put together a lobby strategy that would call attention to the association's issues and launched a campaign that highlighted the value of public transit in Canada.

Early in the campaign, it became apparent that it would be necessary to contact MPs directly and to leverage contacts on Parliament Hill to set up meetings with the people who could bring about change. Documents were designed to help the

Chapter 6.

Ministers
and Their
Offices

association's members advocate serious investment in Canada's mass transit systems.

During the campaign various techniques were used in order to capture the attention of key decision makers. These tactics included:

- Grassroots lobbying that called on CUTA's 100 transit system members

- Biannual advocacy days on the Hill

- Regular meetings with MPs and senior government officials

- Lobby kits that included advocacy briefing papers and meeting guides, all available electronically to members as part of the association's website

- VIP transit symposiums for members of CUTA and politicians

In addition to the extensive lobby days organized, CUTA coordinated multiple photo-ops with key decision-makers. For an interesting twist, association members brought their own buses as transportation for a meeting with the Minister of Public Works and the Minister of the Environment. This was a break-from-the-clutter initiative, which certainly made an impact on Parliament Hill and branded CUTA with all MPs.

It became apparent over the course of the campaign that CUTA was becoming more respected and recognized as an association. As the years went on, the size of the lobby days grew, and cabinet ministers were eager to meet with the public transit executives.

Eventually, newspapers started filling with articles of funding announcements and other initiatives related to mass transit systems. The *Globe and Mail* even went so far as to print that CUTA's grassroots lobby efforts were a key element in gaining federal support for urban transit—a sentiment shared by Michael Roschlau, President and CEO of CUTA.

In the 2006 budget, the Conservative government set aside $1.3 billion in support of public transit infrastructure.

2008—A Streamlined and Intensified Campaign

With success at the federal level for transit remaining strong, CUTA sought to achieve its ultimate goal of substantial funding for national transit programs. After CUTA's intensive lobby effort, the Conservative government also launched the new tax exemption for transit passes for 2006, which was a major victory for the association.

It was apparent that transit was becoming front-and-centre at the federal level. In his speech during the CUTA annual conference in Halifax in June 2007, the minister of transport announced his commitment to the development of a National Transit Strategy. In the second-last week of session in 2007, the House of Commons held a six-hour debate on the federal gas tax with municipalities and focused on urban transit issues. The lengthy debate, as well as the minister's commitment, highlights how far CUTA had come in a few years and shows how well MPs from all parties understood and supported transit issues.

CUTA saw an opportunity to intensify the campaign prior to the tabling of the federal budget on February 26, 2008. The association kicked the campaign into full gear by incorporating the following elements:

- A bus-board advertising campaign

- The development of the National Transit Forum

- An extensive lobby day

- The distribution of bimonthly issue papers and Forum magazines to keep MPs informed of the issues facing the industry

Transit Awareness Days included an awards luncheon where select MPs were recognized for their role in advancing urban transportation initiatives. CUTA officials held meetings with MPs from all provinces, various cabinet ministers, as well as transportation critics from all sides of the House of Commons.

Chapter 6.

Ministers
and Their
Offices

The National Transit Forum acted to further the strategic approach to the continued development and support of transit in Canada. Key participants who attended the National Transit Forum on February 13, 2008 included:

- Federal government representatives

- Provincial & territorial government representatives

- CUTA executive committee members, senior staff, stakeholders and transit suppliers

- CUTA Transit Board Members Committee (municipal elected representatives)

Through the extensive public affairs efforts and advocacy campaigns, CUTA has been working toward a cleaner and greener Canada. More funding for public transit means a better Canada for all of us. The overwhelming success of this campaign means more than just the bottom line; it means that the association has successfully made our government aware of the importance of public transportation in our environment and in Canada's future.

As for funding, this number has gone up considerably—from nothing to over $5 billion in 10 years. A true accomplishment!

Lobbying Municipal Governments

Influencing the actions of municipal governments has taken on increased importance in recent years. Not only has the creation of mega-cities expanded the impact of municipal governments but there is also an increasing recognition that cities are key transmission points for the global economy.

However, it is important to remember when dealing with municipal issues that city governments have no guaranteed constitutional position. Unlike the federal and provincial governments, municipal governments exercise responsibilities set out under provincial authority and specific provincial legislation. Provincial governments also determine the revenue sources available to municipal governments and have ultimate authority for determining the organizational structure of municipal bodies.

In many provinces, there is a significant restructuring underway in terms of the allocation of responsibilities between provincial and municipal governments. As a result, it is important to research and understand fully the role of the provincial government in influencing and regulating local advocacy issues. This is particularly critical to remember given that these powers can differ greatly across provinces.

Another core distinction to consider when dealing municipal government versus federal or provincial bodies is the lack of formal political accountability for local elected officials. Generally speaking, municipal councils operate as a collection of individuals where each individual councillor has his or her own accountability to the electorate. With a few exceptions of Canada's largest cities there is no Government or Official Opposition within local council.

Chapter 7.

Lobbying Municipal Governments

Municipal Decision Makers

The Mayor

There is a public perception that city mayors are responsible for carrying out the role of the chief political executive.

This perception is increased by the fact that mayors are elected at large and there is a sense that they are the city's leader. However, it is the council that has the delegated grant of legislative authority and it is the council that holds the power of formal decision making.

While a mayor's formal power may be more limited than a chief executive officer, there is no doubt that he or she can play a key role in the policy making process. This power extends from the fact that a mayor is often seen to represent the entire city.

A mayor with a strong leadership style and dynamic personality can play the pivotal role in city government. Most importantly, if there is an issue of high public profile, the mayor can play the role of influential policy maker by shaping the debate in the media, lobbying councillors, and leading public opinion. This role does not mean that the city council is accountable to the mayor or vice versa.

In this context, advocacy groups must view the mayor as an important part of the public-policy process but not as the final decision maker. Mayors can be powerful allies or formidable foes but Canadian mayors do not have the same powers at their disposal as their American counterparts.

Council

City councils are generally made up of individuals who are elected in wards or zones within a given municipality. The elected council has responsibility for both the legislative and executive functions. This means that a council must find a way to balance these two very distinct roles.

With the legislative function, most councils are at ease creating a wide variety of policy and program decisions such as by-laws and other regulatory matters. Councillors must set out the rules for everything from parking regulations, to public smoking laws to the frequency of garbage collection.

It is the administrative oversight role that is more difficult for councillors to manage. To overcome this, most cities attempt to establish a link between council and the administrative departments and agencies, generally through standing or special committees. Standing committees usually deal with ongoing functional responsibilities such as transportation or parks and recreation. Special committees are set up to deal with specific issues that are not within the mandate of standing committees or are related to special short-term objectives.

The heads of various municipal departments and agencies generally report to a standing committee on issues relating to their sector. Many larger cites now also have standing committees with such titles as Executive Committee, Policy Committee, or Management Committee. Historically, most of these committees lack major decision-making authority because of the reluctance of the council at large to delegate substantive powers.

Given the important roles that councillors play in both establishing policy and overseeing municipal administration, they are key players in any advocacy campaign aimed at the local level.

It cannot be emphasized enough that in most cases, councillors are the ones in the decision-making process that are the most sensitive to local public pressure. Indeed, it can be argued that councillors' primary role is to represent the views of local voters in their ward.

> **Mayors can be powerful allies or formidable foes but Canadian mayors do not have the same powers at their disposal as their American counterparts.**

Chapter 7.

Lobbying Municipal Governments

Chief Administrative Officer

Responsibility for the general management of the administrative organization in most Canadian municipalities is now placed in the hands of a single professional public servant. This individual is most commonly called the chief administrative officer (CAO) but may also have the title of municipal manager, city commissioner, city administrator, city manager or, in the province of Quebec, director general.

In most instances, this position is formally outlined in provincial legislation that provides for a CAO who manages the implementation of policies set down by council, and who manages the day-to-day function of the public service.

Because the roles of policy implementation and policy making can rarely by separated, council and the CAO are constantly sharing information about the potential impact of policy changes and the potential cost associated with different initiatives. As a result, any municipal lobby effort cannot ignore the subtle interplay between the CAO and council. Working to influence both sides of this relationship is critical to the success of any municipal lobby effort.

Department Heads

Larger municipal administrations are organized into numerous departments, each headed by a senior official. These officials tend to be technical experts focused on their own area of responsibility. This allows advocacy groups to identify the municipal official responsible for their area of concern more easily.

It is important to underscore the fact that at the federal and provincial government levels, a minister (an elected representative) acts as the representative head of each department. The absence of ministerial responsibility at the municipal level increases the prominence of each department head. This means that the department head plays a more significant role in the policy-making process, and is more likely to emerge as the spokesperson for specific municipal services or programs. Examples of department heads include the head of transit, social services, planning, or fire services.

Boards

Complicating the roles of city administration is the proliferation of boards and commissions in many municipal governments. These boards are generally made up of appointed representatives and are therefore less responsive to pressure from voters. Historically, boards were created to take the politics out of local issues by having unelected experts or knowledgeable citizens serve to guide aspects of municipal government.

Examples of boards include police commissions, library boards, arena boards and school boards. All of these boards have varying powers and responsibilities across Canada. Critics of boards argue that they reduce accountability and confuse responsibility. It is also argued that they reduce the clarity of responsibility for establishing fiscal priorities.

In an advocacy context, associations must closely study a board's relationship and degree of independence from council. Boards that are statutory have a higher degree of independence. In many cases, councillors can sit as board members and are therefore more influential. Boards that are appointed by council and overseen closely are generally less influential.

Municipal Advocacy Planning

The fundamental principles of association advocacy campaigns remain constant when dealing with all three levels of government. This includes the importance of issue identification, goal setting, and background research.

> **The most important shift to make when working at the municipal level is to recognize the decentralized decision-making process within Canada's cities.**

Chapter 7.

Lobbying Municipal Governments

The most important shift to make when working at the municipal level is to recognize the decentralized decision-making process within Canada's cities. Without central government to focus on, associations must plan campaigns that take into account a wider variety of stakeholders and the different motivations of decision makers. As alluded to earlier, an advocacy presentation aimed at municipal council needs to reflect arguments that play strongly to the impact on local voters, while presentations made to department heads or chief administrators must be more focused on technical merit and financial factors.

As always, the local media is a significant factor in shaping municipal debates. Associations need to play close attention to media relations that involve local radio talk shows, community newspapers, and newspaper columnists on the city hall beat (more on media relations in Chapter 8).

Municipal Issues on the National Stage

There is an increasing trend in Canada for urban issues to have a higher profile within the national policy framework. Not only are groups such as the Federation of Canadian Municipalities (FCM) increasingly calling for the federal government to establish revenue sharing options to support municipal responsibilities, there is also a shift in thinking at the national level that recognizes the enormous social and economic impact municipal policy has on Canadians.

As a result, many national associations are now actively involved in managing advocacy efforts dealing with several levels of government. The recent lobby effort of the Canadian Urban Transit Association (CUTA), is perhaps the best example of managing multi-pronged campaigns (see the case study at the end of chapter 6 for details).

CUTA has pressed hard at both the federal and provincial levels for increased funding for urban transit which is, of course, a municipal issue. At the same time, however, CUTA has paid careful attention to the influence of FCM and the importance of keeping FCM informed about the importance of the transit case. CUTA needs to ensure that all three levels of government move in harmony towards increased support for urban transit. Not an easy task!

Another example of national associations connecting on urban policy debate is the creation of the Toronto Financial Services Alliance. This group's aim is to highlight the importance of Toronto in the financial service industry on a national and international level. Several national trade associations such as the Canadian Bankers Association and the Canadian Life and Health Insurance Association participate in this alliance. Both of these groups have a long tradition of dealing with national and provincial issues; addressing industry concerns at the municipal level is a definite shift in approach that reflects the increased emphasis on the urban agenda.

TIP FROM THE TRENCHES: From a City Mayor's Point of View

City of Ottawa mayor Jim Watson has a unique perspective on the subtleties of lobbying at the municipal level. In addition to being a big-city mayor, Watson served six years as a municipal councillor and, at the federal level, he served as a senior political assistant to the Speaker of the House of Commons.

Chapter 7.

**Lobbying
Municipal
Governments**

Watson highlights the following points as key
when associations lobby municipal government:

☐ *Municipal governments have a very decentralized
political process. Remember that each councillor has
an important independent vote.*

☐ *Mayors can play an important role in moving issues
forward if they have the support of a block of
councillors. Often a mayor that is effective can be
counted on to deliver several votes on council.*

☐ *Ensure you have the support of local community
associations. These groups are very influential with
council and have torpedoed many wide-scale lobby
efforts.*

☐ *It is important to touch base with the
neighbourhood and not to be secretive. Efforts to
get local voter support can be very important.*

☐ *The saying "all politics is local" is more important at
the municipal level than any other level. Remember
that a group of 20 to 25 people calling a councillor's
office will have a bigger impact at the municipal
level than group calling a federal MP.*

☐ *Committees of council are very important. Not only
are these the place where a lot of work gets done
but they can often be the only place where interest
groups can speak publicly on advocacy issues.*

☐ *Associations need to be careful to remember that
even if an issue is passed at the committee level it
may not pass council. It is important that advocacy
groups never let their guard down.*

Media

Chapter 8.

Media

In any government relations effort, it is critical never to underestimate the power of the media. As seen in the diagram in Chapter 2, politicians and officials closely track media coverage on any given issue and the nature of the press coverage affects these decision makers. The media serves as a measure of public concern regarding government policy. As a result, media coverage inevitably shapes the political agenda.

The best illustration of the impact of media coverage involves a quick overview of how closely politicians and senior officials analyze it. Every morning, a detailed report of the previous day's media coverage is prepared for every department. These media clippings are widely distributed, read, analyzed. They drive a morning procedure known as "tactics," where strategies are devised for responding to, avoiding, and anticipating the fallout from what is said in the media.

Given the significant influence of the media, associations cannot ignore media relations as an essential component of any advocacy approach. It is important to note, however, that media coverage is not always beneficial to an association's lobby efforts; the decision to use media must be carefully examined.

Media Relations Campaigns

As in government relations, there is no substitute for starting early and taking a proactive approach to dealing with the media. This is critical because in many cases, the media define the issue before it hits the political level. As a starting point, it is important not to overlook trade magazines and industry-specific publications when starting a lobby campaign. These publications can play an important role in keeping association members informed on your advocacy efforts and can also ensure that members understand the work of their association.

Trade Press

Trade magazine or industry-specific articles can be used as a way of demonstrating to policy makers that the concerns of an association are well-known across the industry. Leverage your relationship with trade magazines to help government officials better use these publications to reach your audience. Send articles of interest from trade magazines to government officials and politicians, especially if these articles are flattering. They make an excellent opportunity to talk with political leaders.

Specialized Reporters

Associations should familiarize themselves with beat reporters. Employed by mainstream media outlets, these reporters are assigned special focuses or *beats* and so might have a particular interest in your issue or industry. Examples include auto, city, health, and business reporters. Get to know your beat reporters. Have coffee with them or take them to lunch. Continue to send them stories and be prepared to work with them. Beat reporters are a great asset in helping the association get out its message.

Press Gallery

Most political jurisdictions in Canada have a specialized press corps that track and write about daily political events. Whether it is the local city hall beat, the provincial legislature press gallery, or the Parliamentary Press Gallery in Ottawa, these reporters are an influential group in the policy and political process.

Chapter 8.

Media

Gallery reporters often look to outside interest groups for "reaction clips" to accompany the larger story. Having these reporters familiar with your organization provides a greater probability of being contacted for a reaction. Every 30-second sound bite is free publicity for you, your organization, and its members. A list of gallery reporters can usually be obtained by contacting the press gallery office in the respective legislature.

TIP FROM THE TRENCHES: Make it Newsworthy

"Recognize that smaller newsrooms and multi-tasking now means reporters have precious little time. Your event may be important to your association, but that doesn't it make it news. Know what the reporters' responsibilities are. If you can, tailor your pitch so that it sounds like news rather than a calendar item."

Rob Russo, Ottawa Bureau Chief Canadian Press and CBC At Issue Panelist

Local Media

The role of local press can also be important in influencing the mind set of a political leader. The MP from Calgary will pay special attention to political columns in the *Calgary Herald*, while a minister from Toronto might pay considerable attention to media coverage in the *Toronto Star*. Associations need to consider these factors when combining media relations and advocacy strategies.

Community newspapers, radio stations, and television channels are a great resource for associations trying to advance a message. These media are often short on news content and welcome potential stories from interest groups. In particular, community newspapers provide access to a vast readership and can play a key role in influencing local opinion. If you are trying to influence particular decision makers, doing it in their own backyard is very effective.

Building and Maintaining Media Relationships

Associations should also understand that sustained media coverage is difficult to achieve. The very nature of the media is to cover what is hot and new as opposed to detailed policy analysis. The media is looking for conflict and opposing views. Whether staging a news conference or sending a press release, associations should always consider the most fundamental concern of both reporters and editors: is this really newsworthy?

Getting the Media's Attention

Press Release

The most common method of attracting the media's attention is to distribute a press release. The advent of modern communications technology means that this can now be achieved by broadcast email.

A good press release should grab attention and contain the entire story. Think of the popular political commentary show W5 and answer the five basis questions: who, what, where, when, and why? Also, imagine the press release as a pyramid with your opening statement addressing the point of your release and additional paragraphs providing more information and widening the base.

What is your key message? Be succinct and write for your audience. Ask yourself if the journalist really needs that information. Is it relevant?

Use appropriate language. If your audience is the mainstream media and you're trying to reach the average person, don't use language that only you and your members understand. Try to avoid acronyms and terms that are specific to your industry.

> **Use appropriate language. If your audience is the mainstream media and you're trying to reach the average person, don't use language that only you and your members understand.**

Chapter 8.
Media

The best quotes are short, memorable, and relevant. Include the name and title of the person providing the quote.

Finally, provide a contact person and number in case the journalists require additional information.

Media Kit

Another standard tool that can complement an advocacy campaign is the media kit. These kits can be an excellent means of providing editors and reporters with the full background on an association's public policy issue. A media kit can include a press release, background information, a relevant photo, and additional information on the issues, members, industry facts, and the association in general.

Editorial Board Meetings

An association meeting with newspaper editorial boards is an important step in explaining an association position on complicated advocacy files. Editorial board meetings are on-the-record meetings between senior association representatives and the editorial staff of a newspaper. In addition to relevant editors, reporters are usually present. The format is usually an hour-long, free-flowing discussion of an issue affecting the association. Newspapers usually accept a proposed editorial board meeting when there is an issue that has high-profile ramifications for public policy.

Offer your organization's willingness to participate in an editorial board meeting by writing to the editor of the respective newspaper. In addition, inform the beat reporters or your contacts at the newspaper of your organization's interest in participating and solicit their assistance in arranging the opportunity. Editorial boards can be high-pressure situations; I recommend that associations should have advanced levels of media experience if they plan to use editorial boards to get their message out.

Special Events

A popular means of generating media coverage and providing a backdrop for an association's media message is the special event, including a press conference. Given recent reductions in reporting staffs, the media will not necessarily cover routine meetings such as conferences and trade shows. As noted earlier, even if the association's members consider an event to be important, this does not mean the media will cover it.

Special events to capture media attention include the kick-off of an advocacy campaign, a protest action, or the announcement of research findings or polling results. An advocacy event at city hall or a special association session on Parliament Hill can also draw media coverage.

TIP FROM THE TRENCHES: On Political Media Events

Parliament Hill, many provincial legislatures, and some city halls provide access to media studios or media gathering points so that associations can hold press events aimed at the political press. These studio arrangements provide associations with a ready-made backdrop for delivering an important public policy message to the press and elected officials. Many political offices monitor these press events closely and in some jurisdictions there are live television feeds to elected offices and all news bureaus. Before using one of these facilities, make sure that your message is both timely and relevant to political media.

Chapter 8.

Media

Monitoring the Enemy

In any advocacy campaign that pits your association against another, closely monitor the media activities of opposing organizations. In an adversarial environment it is important to be prepared to leave "no shot unanswered." Aggressive media and advocacy plans must include contingencies to respond to attacks.

CHECKLIST: Rules for Handling the Press

☐ *Establish the terms of an interview at the beginning. There is no such thing as "off the record."*

☐ *Agree on one spokesperson who will speak for the organization.*

☐ *Be prepared. Know your subject thoroughly before meeting with the journalist. Prior to the interview, create a set of no more than three key messages you want to get across. Practise delivering them aloud.*

☐ *Establish your association's key messages and keep coming back to them throughout the interview.*

☐ *Never lie to reporters even about mundane details such as why you cannot take their call.*

☐ *Understand media deadlines and make every attempt to help meet them.*

☐ *Most journalists like to ask difficult questions, so be prepared for them.*

☐ *Take control of the interview. While the journalist asking the questions would appear to control the interview, you can steer the course of the session by returning to key messages.*

☐ *Keep your own record of the interview. Make an audio or video recording of your comments. This will assist you in practising your delivery and will also serve as insurance against being wrongly quoted.*

☐ *Remember, the media will always have the last word.*

Noisy Toys

The Canadian Association of Speech-Language Pathologists and Audiologists (CASLPA) sought to launch a proactive advocacy campaign in September 2006. CASLPA wanted to alert parents and caregivers to the potential dangers of noisy toys to their child's hearing in anticipation of the upcoming holiday shopping season. This message was an essential step in preventing harm to a child's hearing, which can lead to serious communication and learning difficulties. In addition to the warning, CASLPA sought to raise awareness of speech-language pathologists and audiologists, and to raise the profile of the association. Most importantly, CASLPA wanted to leverage this public awareness into legislative action.

Challenges

Due to the somewhat technical nature of the message—the interpretation of noise levels in decibels—the messages could appear too complicated to understand. The association had to simplify the communication enough so that parents and caregivers would recognize its importance, but to maintain the technical, measurable criteria that validates the message.

Strategy/Tactics

Simplifying the message was indispensable in creating a bigger impact on the public and politicians. The following points were outlined in the press conference and were explained in detail in a background document that was made available to the media.

- "How loud is too loud?" is the obvious question when warning of noisy toys. CASLPA brought a noisy toy to the press conference, which was used as a demonstration. Providing viewers with a concrete example of what a noisy toy sounds like created a frame of reference for parents.

- Helpful tips on how to tell if a toy is too loud were outlined.

- Audiologists recommended safety tips to consider when buying toys, in an effort to warn parents and consumers on the dangers that some noisy toys have.

Chapter 8.

Media

In order to publicize the message, the following methods were used.

- A national press conference was held at the National Press Gallery in Ottawa.

- Media advisories were sent to 552 media outlets across Canada. As a follow-up, dozens of journalists were directly contacted and encouraged to attend the press conference.

- Letters were sent to MPs with a detailed background document to explain the message.

Reference was made to Health Canada's strict guidelines for noise produced by toys, and to the fact that research and real-life experience show a disregard for these guidelines. CASLPA demonstrated how children often bring toys close to their faces and ears even though the toy was designed to be held further away from the body. It was clearly illustrated how the regulation will not always protect children's hearing. It was also noted that many toys are innocently brought into Canada as gifts from a foreign country and therefore never get tested to Canadian standards.

As a result of the press conference, the event received a vast amount of media coverage: TV and radio news stations reported the event throughout the day during their live broadcasts. The message was featured on many networks' 6 p.m. and 11 p.m. news broadcasts. Major news stations, newspapers, and all major media outlets were interested in the message. CASLPA representatives had so many requests for interviews that they were booked solid for days following the press conference. CASLPA achieved the most comprehensive media coverage of any event in the association's history:

- Close to 5 million Canadians (over 14% of the population) saw the message.

- There was coverage in print news, with circulation totals of over 340,000.

- TV and radio hits were extremely impressive, reaching approximately 4,425,000 Canadians (13% of Canadians).

Ultimately, the media pressure led to political action in a perfect blend of media and advocacy strategy. MP Judy Wasylycia-Leis invited CASLPA to attend a national press conference on Parliament Hill where she announced the tabling of her private member's bill in support of CASLPA's initiatives. This was a great use of opposition MP support. More recently, Health Canada introduced regulations regarding noise emissions for children's toys, lowering the acceptable level of emissions as per CASLPA's request.

Grassroots Lobbying

Chapter 9.

Grassroots Lobbying

Grassroots lobbying has long been the central focus of advocacy in the United States. Associations and ad hoc coalitions have traditionally relied on mobilizing members to deliver lobby messages to key legislators. Canadian associations have, by contrast, relied more on association staff and board members to deliver a more centralized lobby message to ministers and senior officials. As we have seen, while associations play a key role in communicating member concerns to government through a coordinated advocacy approach, elected officials still respond best to local pressure.

Association members can play a key role in advancing the association's goals by interacting with elected officials directly—and associations can facilitate such meetings by establishing grassroots lobby programs.

Over the past decade, Canadian associations have begun leveraging technology to deliver highly effective grassroots lobby campaigns. The fundamental principle behind the success of grassroots lobbying is that elected officials respond more directly to the concerns of voters and organizations in their local riding than they do to generic advocacy messages.

American Tip O'Neil, the long-time Speaker of the House of Representatives, summed this up best when he coined the phrase "all politics is local." Canadian officials are increasingly shaped by voices from their own constituency. As advocacy campaigns unfold, it is important to keep members informed with ongoing advocacy updates and bulletins in association publications and websites. An informed membership is an empowered membership.

Additionally, information about regulatory and legislative changes is one of the most visible and valued services for most association members. Analysis of government issues, articles on government trends and interviews of government officials all have high value as part of association publications. In many cases, in-depth reports on legislative and regulatory changes are a primary reason to join trade associations.

The Advantages of the Grassroots Approach for Associations

The advantages of a grassroots approach for member-based associations are clear:

- Association members are fully informed and involved in the advocacy efforts of the group. Generally speaking, an informed and active member is more likely to stay committed to the association.

- An active grassroots approach brings the association staff into closer contact with the concerns of the members. Grassroots lobbying involves a two-way flow of communication between the members and the association.

- Increased membership recruitment opportunities and advocacy efforts reach more members and potential members.

- Grassroots lobby campaigns increase member involvement and a commitment to association work.

Keys to Grassroots Success

- Effective association lobbying relies on membership involvement.

- Grassroots communications of concerns has the greatest impact on local representatives.

> " Elected officials respond more directly to the concerns of voters and organizations in their local riding than they do to generic advocacy messages. "

Chapter 9.

Grassroots
Lobbying

- Broad-based communication should support a central message.
- Originality is needed to break through the clutter!
- A sustained and coordinated approach should be managed centrally but applied locally.
- Personalized approaches to elected officials work best— real people explaining real problems to officials, guided by association kits.
- Feedback from member letters and visits is critical.

How the Grassroots Association Member Can Be Effective with Elected Officials

Conversations with Elected Officials

As an individual association member talking to an elected official in your riding (or ward), you should be prepared with:

- Local statistics that apply to the riding or ward
- Real-life stories and examples that illustrate the local case
- A description of your own visibility and profile in the area
- Specific actions that will make you happy

Meeting With Your MP

In a meeting with an MP, you should bring:

- Only one or two key arguments
- A very short, personal story
- A specific request
- Concise leave-behind material
- A thank-you note

Effective Letters to MPs

As part of a grassroots advocacy program, a good letter to an MP should:

- State up front that you are a constituent

- Provide a street address in the riding
- Lead with your request
- Speak from the heart
- Contain one core argument
- Avoid big packages of information
- Repeat the request
- Can be typed or hand-written (but must be legible)
- Should be copied to your association

Effective and Powerful Grassroots Email

If an email is a better option, keep in mind:

- Email delivers speed but implies a lack of investment
- It's even more important to signal you are a constituent
- Your subject line should be clear, e.g., Message from Red Deer
- Include your mailing address in first line
- Personalize the request
- Avoid attachments
- Avoid spam

Compelling Telephone Calls to Local MPs

When time is a factor, using the phone might be the best option:

- Identify that you are a constituent
- Provide your mailing address
- Brief the staffer, who is a great source of information and action
- Ask for a return call by the MP
- Do not call on every issue—reserve the political capital

Chapter 9.

Grassroots Lobbying

Grassroots Tactics that Don't Work

- Contact that looks purely bought by mass pressure

- A confrontational style that harasses or insults the official

- Being under-informed or speaking without conviction

- Not having have the tools to lobby, or appearing too rehearsed or artificial

- Lack of preparedness

- Not listening

The Importance of Grassroots Political Fundraising

Political fundraising is one of the cornerstones of our democracy and a critical part of effective grassroots political lobbying. Fundraising stands out as a unique commitment to support candidates in a way that is critical to their success.

Instead of mailing a cheque, consider attending a fundraiser and meeting the candidate and political staff. Or, even better, maximize your fundraising influence by hosting a fundraising event with local small-business leaders or individuals in your circle of influence.

You can also host an informal meeting in your home or office, advising the politician of your intent to donate to the campaign after the meeting. This gives you a chance to get to know the politician and familiarize him or her with you. Don't give money all at once. When a donation amount is decided upon, it is effective to give it in stages: before, during and after the election.

In the Canadian context, there are several excellent examples of associations harnessing the power of the grassroots to achieve government relations success. In the following example, targeting the media and the individual MPs directly were important parts of the campaign, but the grassroots involvement by the association's members was instrumental to achieving their goal.

A $12 Billion Dollar Success

The Canadian Automobile Dealers Association (CADA) is a well-organized and sophisticated association representing over 3,000 franchised new car and truck dealers across Canada. According to CADA president Richard Gauthier, the association specializes in "leveraging the role dealers play in their local community to advance our advocacy agenda." Targeting is critical. "We cannot afford the resources to always contact every dealer on every issue, so it is important for us to be able to take a surgical approach when mobilizing members," added Gauthier.

CADA has a state-of-the-art membership system that breaks down members by both federal and provincial ridings. Beyond that, detailed political survey results help the association establish which members have the best relationship with local politicians. CADA tracks everything from local fundraising to personal contacts with elected and unelected officials.

During the fall of 2008, when the global economy started showing signs of distress, every sector of the automotive industry was feeling an extreme credit crunch. Dealers, each of whom relies on millions of dollars of credit to finance floor plans and operations, were being blocked by the banks, whose lending had frozen— leaving them without access to the capital they required to run their business. Also, manufacturers were in desperate need of support in order to preserve jobs and keep business afloat.

CADA's over 3,000 dealers represent a vital sector of Canada's economy, employing over 140,000 people across the country in virtually every community. Among the association's numerous roles, CADA works with the federal government on issues that affect the retail sector of the automobile industry and works to improve relations between dealers and manufacturers.

On behalf of its member dealers and the auto industry as a whole, CADA led the way in a targeted lobbying campaign to underscore to the Canadian public and policy makers that the auto industry is the engine of the entire country's economy and not just that of a single province. (The auto industry is the largest contributor to Canada's manufacturing gross domestic product and is responsible for one in seven jobs nationwide.)

Chapter 9.

Grassroots Lobbying

Start with the Media

On November 21, 2008, CADA held a national press conference on Parliament Hill with a clear message about the need for proactive and aggressive federal policies to aid the auto industry in Canada. This strategy sought to leverage media in order to gain political attention and action—an essential part of advocacy, as we saw in Chapter 8.

To a room filled with representatives from every Canadian news outlet, CADA emphasized that the automotive manufacturing downturn would have a ripple effect in every community in Canada and that the cold reality facing decision makers was that if Canadian-based manufacturers were not provided a bridge across the economic crisis, then Canada's 3,500 small business dealers, located in every community of the country, would bear the brunt of the downturn.

As in the previous case study on urban transit, the media coverage of the press conference was unprecedented, with CADA's phone lines flooded with interview requests. In the days following the announcement, CADA appeared on every broadcast network across the country, including high profile interviews on CBC Newsworld and Mike Duffy Live. The association's representatives also acted as the voice of the industry on radio stations from coast to coast and appeared in print publications on national and local levels, totalling over 200 media interviews.

Galvanize the Effort Nation-Wide

Following the press conference, CADA launched a massive grassroots advocacy initiative wherein dealers in communities across Canada contacted their MPs to urge the government to increase liquidity and provide financing to the manufacturer's finance companies of all brands. During the campaign, the association held satellite video broadcasts across the country to inform the membership and mobilize local lobby efforts.

Next, CADA contacted senior cabinet ministers, including the Minister of Finance, Jim Flaherty, to outline auto dealer credit concerns and measures to increase lending capacity. Additionally, CADA contacted the Minister of Industry, Tony

Clement, in early December to press the association's priorities, followed by meetings with senior finance officials to outline credit and liquidity concerns with the officials responsible for implementing government initiatives in credit markets.

On December 20, 2008, CADA President and CEO Richard Gauthier was front and centre when Prime Minister Stephen Harper and Ontario Premier Dalton McGuinty pledged financial support to help Canadian automakers with their operations. The announcement revealed the Government of Canada's and the Government of Ontario's commitment to provide $4 billion in loans payable to General Motors of Canada Ltd. and Chrysler Canada Inc., through Export Development Canada (EDC). His presence was a key strategic element to demonstrate broad small business support for the government's action and was an important interim step of saying thank you to the government.

With the momentum of the December 20 announcement, CADA stayed focused on the goal of alleviating the credit crunch for its member dealers. In anticipation of the 2009 federal budget, CADA formed a strategic partnership with the Canadian Finance and Leasing Association (CFLA), and brought a proposal to the Ministry of Finance that consisted of an injection of liquidity for non-bank lenders through an asset purchase, very similar to what the government had done for banks with its multi-billion dollar mortgage purchase commitment. Again, strategic partnerships can be critical for association advocacy success.

On January 27, 2009, in its 2009 Federal Budget, the Government of Canada announced a new $12 billion program designed to address the shortage of liquidity and credit for the automotive industry and its consumers. A full section of the budget was dedicated to the auto industry and the Government pledged to create the Canadian Secured Credit Facility with allocations of up to $12 billion to purchase term asset-backed securities (ABS) backed by loans and leases on vehicles. CADA's targeted campaign proved extremely successful as the measures outlined in the budget answered squarely CADA's call to provide liquidity to auto dealers and consumers and would help to unfreeze credit markets and allow the affiliate finance companies to support dealers and consumers..

Chapter 9.

Grassroots Lobbying

Grassroots Lobbying Concepts to Consider

Action Bulletin

A letter, fax, email, or phone call from an association to members designed to provide information on key issues and mobilize members.

Bounce-back

A direct mail response system, often a pre-printed postage-paid card that is completed by association members to provide feedback on their local lobby activities.

Database Matches

A system of matching association members, addresses, and postal codes with municipal, provincial, or federal election districts. This powerful tool allows associations to target grassroots activity closely.

Interactive Kiosk

An exhibit booth at a convention, trade show, or association conference where members use a computer terminal to transmit electronic concerns to politicians or officials.

Satellite Conferencing

An electronic broadcast or meeting to inform members and mobilize activity. This approach can also be used to put a group of constituents in contact with a politician to discuss a legislative issue.

Telephone Patch-Through

A means of contacting association members by telephone and, if agreeable, connecting them directly with the targeted politician's office so they can deliver a personal advocacy message.

More Key Ingredients to Consider

Research for Advocacy

As governments feel the pressure of resource constraints, associations have an opportunity to fill the information void by providing officials with research to help them make informed policy decisions. In many cases, this information is readily available as a core part of the association's existing activities. As a result, the information simply needs to be repackaged to serve as the basis for advocacy material.

Governments are far more likely to respond favourably to an advocacy campaign based on solid, well-researched facts and arguments. This is especially true given the mounting pressure on the capacity of governments to undertake expensive research. Surveys, economic reports and the expertise of members can be extremely important tools. Credible and well-documented arguments build an association's long-term credibility with government. Submissions that appear manipulative or deceptive can torpedo an association's relationship with government for years.

Several successful associations make use of their annual reports or year-end industry analysis as the basis for keeping policy makers informed. Even the simple step of mailing these updates can play an important role in shaping government's understanding of an association's members. Follow-up meetings or telephone calls to review these reports can add value to the information exchange.

> " Several successful associations make use of their annual reports or year-end industry analysis as the basis for keeping policy makers informed. "

Chapter 10.

More Key Ingredients to Consider

In many cases, associations need to respond to specific government requests for information. Often, these requests are part of the policy development process and provide an opportunity for associations to serve members by informing government.

Polling Your Members

Associations have several means for gathering information from the membership.

Mail Surveys — This is an inexpensive means of gathering data from a large group of members. Mail surveys also offer a high degree of anonymity that increases the likelihood of accurate responses. Associations also need to consider the best hook for attracting member responses. Tying the survey to a specific advocacy campaign is often helpful. The disadvantage is the length of time required to send and receives these surveys.

Fax / Email Surveys — A written survey that is faxed or emailed to members is essentially the same as a mail survey, except that there is generally a shorter response time.

Telephone Surveys — This method provides a quick snapshot of members but can be expensive. Associations also need to be concerned with the possibility that a poorly designed telephone survey can bias results.

Focus Groups — Focus groups are an excellent means of getting members to respond to interactive questions and to engage in detailed brainstorming. Focus groups are less statistically effective in conveying reliable information about an entire association membership to government.

Website Surveys — Website surveys are an efficient way to measure information from regular visitors to an association's home page. However, because of a self-selection bias, it is difficult to draw accurate conclusions from website surveys about an association's entire membership.

Polling Public Opinion

Public opinion is central to the political process and almost
always plays a role in any major advocacy campaign.
Elected and unelected officials alike are sensitive to the
public's perception of issues. Governments spend millions of
dollars every year to poll the public on issues of the day. An
association that is able to demonstrate to government that
their advocacy position has public support therefore has an
advantage.

The major problem with polling is cost. Hiring outside
polling firms to conduct large-scale public opinion polls
makes sense on a large-scale critical campaign. However,
such polling drains financial resources that could be aimed
at other important advocacy activities. Whether financial
resources are limited or not, associations should first consult
existing information sources.

Published data from Statistics Canada, private research
institutions and government departments can often provide
an in-depth overview of public opinion to assist in lobbying
efforts. Association staff who aggressively mine census
reports and other published documents can establish the
foundations of advocacy arguments based on public opinion.

Perhaps the best source of public opinion data is previously
published media polls. In many cases media polls have
tracked public opinion on major policy issues for decades.

If an association determines that a specialized public opinion
poll is necessary, there are several means for working
with well-established survey firms to control costs. Sample
surveys and single questions attached to larger polls can be
beneficial.

Building Research Capacity

Many association leaders believe that successful government
relations campaigns will increasingly rely on credible
background research. Nothing can undercut an association's

Chapter 10.

More Key Ingredients to Consider

credibility with government more than inaccurate research or claims based on faulty assumptions.

Long-term research capabilities are a worthwhile investment. Associations are uniquely placed to be the information centre for their industry sector or membership area. Too often associations fail to see the need for research until faced with a dramatic shift in government policy. Associations that have strong government relations track records usually have made the investment in industry research.

> ### TIP FROM THE TRENCHES:
> ### Researched, Reasoned, Rational
>
> "Whether trying to stop, amend or initiate government action, a thoroughly researched and reasoned policy rationale is the trump card for an effective advocacy campaign."
>
> **Andrew Casey,** Vice President, Public Affairs Forest Products Association

Coalition Building

When making policy decisions, governments have a strong desire for consensus. As a result, associations that can work together to present a unified front to government can often achieve impressive results.

In the cut and thrust of lobbying activities, coalition building is an often-overlooked but highly effective tool. Associations can broaden their reach and awareness by working with groups that have interests that parallel their own. In addition to increased impact, coalitions offer several tangible benefits including shared financing of lobbying activities such as research, advertising, and meeting with officials.

TIP FROM THE TRENCHES:
Work with Others to Achieve More

Mark Nantais, president of the Canadian Vehicle
Manufacturers Association (CVMA) views working with
other associations as an essential part of his advocacy
efforts for the Big Three automakers: "CVMA recognizes
that we can often achieve more with government when
working with other key automotive associations than
working in isolation. If we are fighting an issue that
affects the entire industry, our voice in government
is strong when working in partnership with other
manufacturers' associations, or dealers' associations."

Many association executives have sought to work in
coalitions to take advantage of financial and human
resources. The trade-offs, however, are loss of control
over the advocacy process and increased time demands in
managing cooperative activity. Building and maintaining
consensus in coalitions demands tremendous time and
patience, and can reduce advocacy flexibility.

There are two primary disadvantages to working within
coalitions: first, the increased resources required to plan
and coordinate group activities; and second, the possibility
that the requirements of group consensus will dull an
association's messages and broaden objectives too much to
be effective.

Chapter 10.

More Key Ingredients to Consider

CHECKLIST: Before You Build a Coalition

Before embarking on a coalition it is important to review the following:

☐ *Do the potential partners have a shared vision and shared goals? It is important to define success and get all the coalition players to sign on to this definition before embarking on a coalition.*

☐ *Can the partners agree upon a workable advocacy plan? It is critical that coalition partners clearly outline roles and responsibilities.*

☐ *Are cost-sharing agreements clear and explicit? Many coalitions waste time and energy fighting over cost allocations that should be agreed upon as early as possible.*

☐ *Can the coalition partners take small workable steps in the early stages? By focusing on immediate action, coalitions can more easily demonstrate success to all partners, and ultimately sustain the coalition in the long run.*

☐ *Do the partners have an exit strategy? Each association should know under what terms and conditions they would abandon the coalition. Associations should also have plans to exit the coalition when it has achieved all its goals.*

Government Relations with a Minority Government

Minority governments occur when the leading political party fails to obtain enough seats to hold a majority in the legislative house. This effectively means that the Prime Minister or Premier cannot control the legislative and public policy agenda with the sole support of his own party. On important bills, if the government loses a vote, an election is called. This means leaders must make concessions to at least some of the opposition party members to pass all bills.

Alternatively, the Prime Minister or Premier can take a hard-line approach and hope the opposition does not like the timing of a potential election or that the opposition fails to coordinate votes with other opposition parties.

Given the almost half-decade of minority government at the federal level at the time of printing, I am often asked for the rules of navigating this more complex political environment. Association leaders need to understand how best to navigate minority situations.

As a starting point, the political atmosphere during minority rule is more partisan than during majority rule. The threat of an election is almost constant and as such, almost everything MPs do is a means to a political end.

On a personal level, MPs worry about election implications on every action they take; individual political animosity runs high. In majority situations, MPs settle into a more cooperative mode knowing they will not face an election for up to five years. With a minority government, there is little or no multi-partisan cooperation, which means that agreement on even small policy issues becomes more difficult.

Generally, minority governments last much less time, with an 18-month average. This means that delaying legislation is easier than in majority settings, which are characterized by higher rates of government bill passage. Lobbying for new legislation is harder in minorities because of compressed legislative time frames. Parliamentary prorogation or restarts, more frequent under minorities in the past decade, mean that legislation in progress dies and needs to be reintroduced.

> **During minority governments, it is generally true that department officials wield more influence as they know their political masters have less control and time to implement their political agenda.**

Chapter 10.

More Key Ingredients to Consider

During minority governments, it is generally true that department officials wield more influence as they know their political masters have less control and time to implement their political agenda. Senior officials can leverage political uncertainty to delay new government actions. Many times, seeking a departmental advocacy solution can have more certainty and stability for association lobbyists.

In general, lobbying opposition MPs takes on greater importance during minority governments. In a majority, the government almost always gets its way and does not need the help of any other parties to pass legislation. In a minority, the government always needs the support of at least one other party in the House to get anything done. As a result, opposition MPs become highly relevant in the House and in committees.

Parliamentary committees are always an important forum for government relations work, but are more so in a minority setting. During minority governments, committees hold greater power; many significant shifts in government policy can be obtained at the committee level. Committees are almost always controlled by opposition parties and therefore legislation often changes substantially during the committee process. Every government bill is the subject of much greater legislative negotiation and uncertainty. Lobbying opposition MPs on government bills therefore becomes an important.

Overall, there is a need for a multi-partisan approach during minority situations. Associations need relationships with representatives of all parties. Of course it makes sense to focus more on the governing party, but associations must stress solutions that resonate with all parties.

More than ever, associations must frame advocacy in the public and consumer interest as MPs are more focused on public perception with an ever-looming election. The advocacy side that owns the consumer case has huge advantage and can leverage consumer issues with a reminder of pending elections.

Grass roots activity is key during a minority government. MPs on the edge of an election are looking for the chance to touch base with local association members; they want opportunities to be helpful. Given the increased profile of all MPs in a minority situation, grassroots advocacy work becomes more important. MPs are much more conscious of local impact when facing elections. It is critical that all member-based associations leverage this to their advocacy advantage.

Online Advocacy and Social Media

There is little doubt that the last decade has brought a revolution in the use of the Internet to connect people with groups they belong to or causes they care about. The growth of social networking has accelerated the pace of change. In fact, Canada has one of the highest levels of social networking engagement in the world.

Most associations use the Internet to host the organization's website. This website usually serves as an electronic brochure for important information about the association. Generally, there are also special member sections for more detailed member-only benefits.

What is missing on most association websites is a full suite of advocacy material, which should include association position papers. There should also be member links to the association's draft letters to politicians, frequent updates on advocacy activities and progress, highlights of upcoming advocacy events, and profiles of key political decision makers that impact the association's key issues.

> " Grass roots activity is key during a minority government. MPs on the edge of an election are looking for opportunities to touch base with local association members and want opportunities to be helpful. "

Chapter 10.

More Key Ingredients to Consider

CASE STUDY

Powerful online tools

Recent software advances have allowed associations to use powerful online tools that match local postal codes with email addresses for federal and provincial elected officials. All that is required is for the association members to enter their postal codes online and then with a few clicks send a prepared email to their local representative. The power of this tool comes from how easy it is for members to participate. Five minutes of effort creates an issue-specific email to an MP.

The downside of course is that MPs know that pre-defined emails require much less effort and commitment from constituents. Therefore, while tracking emails for trends, MPs discount the overall impact compared to personalized letters and phone calls. An instructive example of online activism sparked by an association was the recent protest over copyright legislation launched by the Canadian Library Association (CLA) in 2007.

Fair Copyright for Canada on Facebook

The CLA, Canada's largest national library association, provides a broad range of services to 2,300 personal and 500 institutional members, and represents the concerns of some 57,000 individuals who work in library and information services in Canada.

In the fall of 2007, with highly anticipated new copyright legislation expected, more and more librarians were hearing from concerned public-library users that copyright laws must reflect the public interest.

As the voice of library users and professionals, CLA was committed to getting the crucial message to the government that copyright issues do indeed strike a chord with the general public. As a response to the concern of over 21 million library users and member librarians about pending copyright legislation, CLA developed an advocacy effort drawing on traditional and social media awareness.

CLA wanted to publicize its core issues and lobby the government for specifics that it wanted to see in any new copyright legislation. It became apparent that a media event would be the most effective way to communicate this message to the public, while gaining credibility for CLA. The library community's key concerns were also outlined in a letter accompanied by the press release to the Minister of Industry and the Minister of Canadian Heritage, as well as MPs. CLA also released an online advocacy toolkit to oppose the copyright bill.

Dr. Michael Geist, a well-known and respected Canadian law professor at the University of Ottawa who has been a leader in the Canadian copyright campaign, linked CLA's message to his Facebook group, Fair Copyright for Canada. This group was formed to help ensure that the government heard from concerned Canadians. It featured news about the bill, tips on making the public voice heard, and updates on local events. With regular postings and links to other content, this form of new media also provided a central spot for people to learn more about Canadian copyright reform.

As a result of CLA's press release, Dr. Geist featured CLA on his own, often-visited website, as well as on his Facebook group, exposing people across the world to the message, building CLA's profile.

CLA was able to feed into a wave of massive online response. Over 90,000 Canadians joined the Facebook group opposing the copyright bill. Live protests were organized online, including a rally at the Minister of Industry's local constituency office.

The online protest eventually led to the bill being withdrawn—a clear victory for online advocacy.

Conclusion

Any association embarking on a serious government relations program must view the undertaking as a long-term commitment. Excellence in association advocacy is only achieved with a sustained record of success while maintaining the association's overall credibility with governments. Unsuccessful organizations too often make the mistake of compromising their future in pursuit of short-term lobbying success. The role of association leaders is to ensure that the "fog of war" does not cost the association and its members future political clout.

When success is achieved, it is essential that associations give credit to the decision makers who contributed to victory. Politicians and officials are likely to respond most favourably when given credit for their work. Importantly, this sets the stage for future work on different issues.

Too often, groups get what they want from governments and forget to say thank you. This is a cardinal sin in government relations. It is also important not to burn bridges after a lobbying defeat. The most successful associations are as professional in defeat as they are in victory.

Finally, it bears repeating that the most effective government relations strategies involve laying groundwork and putting building blocks in place so that the association can forge relationships with decision makers before they are confronted with a government relations crisis. Given the historical importance of advocacy work to the vast majority of association members, it is critical that sufficient resources are assigned to government relations activities. This investment will, in the long run, greatly benefit the association and its members.

Appendix A

Government Relations Checklist

- ☐ *Be proactive. Start early and shape government policy.*

- ☐ *Develop a formal government relations plan that includes member input.*

- ☐ *Be persistent and follow up with officials after making contact. The best advocacy approach involves educating and sensitizing decision makers over time.*

- ☐ *Increase the profile of the association. Associations that are seen publicly to be the voice of their sector are more likely to be consulted by government before policy changes are implemented.*

- ☐ *Be visible and accessible to officials and elected politicians.*

- ☐ *Involve members in advocacy efforts. Even modest efforts at grassroots mobilization can pay big dividends.*

- ☐ *Understand the role of the media in shaping public policy. Develop plans for dealing with the media.*

- ☐ *Review advocacy efforts regularly. Plans need to adapt to the changing environment.*

- ☐ *Be patient.*

- ☐ *Say Thank You!*

Appendix B

Some Lobbying Do's

☐ **Do target your advocacy work to key decision makers on a direct and personal basis.** *Nothing works better than direct personal contact with rational face-to-face presentations and discussion in a private setting.*

☐ **Do demonstrate broad support among association members and, if possible, the general public.** *Anything you can do to demonstrate the support of the community is given a great deal of credibility at the political level.*

☐ **Do remain calm.** *Never become frustrated or angry when a politician or official does not immediately agree with your position. Success depends on the ability to change opinions during a potentially extended policy debate.*

☐ **Do express genuine disagreement.** *Polite displays of emotion can go a long way to demonstrating the sincerity of the advocacy message.*

☐ **Do keep the door open.** *Burning bridges with political leaders or officials is never a good idea. In the advocacy arena, supporters can shift and differ from issue to issue. It is critical to maintain good relationships and not alienate a potential future ally.*

Appendix C

Correspondence Guidelines for Politicians and Government Officials

When writing to politicians and/or government officials in Canada, the following formats are acceptable.

Prime Minister
The Right Honourable John Smith
Prime Minister of Canada
House of Commons
Ottawa, Ontario
K1A 0A6
Dear Prime Minister:

Federal Cabinet Ministers
The Honourable John Smith
Minister of Finance
<Insert Address>
Dear Minister:

Federal MPs
Mr. John Smith, M.P., riding name
<Insert Address>
Dear Mr. Smith:

Premier (example, Ontario)
The Honourable Jane Smith
Premier of Ontario
Legislative Buildings
Queen's Park
Toronto, Ontario M7A 1A2
Dear Premier:

Provincial Cabinet Ministers
The Honourable Jane Smith
Minister of Tourism
<Insert Address>
Dear Minister:

Provincial MPPs/MLAs
Ms. Jane Smith, M.P.P., riding name
<Insert Address>
Dear Ms. Smith:

Mayor
Mayor John Smith
Mayor's Office, City Hall
<Insert Address>
Dear Mayor Smith:

Councillors
Councillor John Smith
City Hall
<Insert Address>
Dear Councillor Smith

Note that correspondence to the House of Commons in Ottawa does not require postage but letters sent to provincial and municipal governments do. Letters to federal politicians require postage when the address does not include the House of Commons.

About the Author

Huw Williams is the President of Impact Public Affairs and is a nationally recognized expert on advocacy and strategic communications for not-for-profit associations and industry trade groups. He is a trusted advisor to scores of leading national and provincial associations, helping them achieve their government relations and public affairs objectives.

Williams' advocacy and communications expertise are based on solid practical experience. Prior to forming Impact Public Affairs, Williams was the Director of Public Affairs for a national industry association. Williams also served in several senior advisory roles for leading cabinet ministers.

In 2006, Mr. Williams was recognized by the Ottawa Business Journal with the "Top Forty Under Forty Award" for professional success and community involvement. In 2009, he was named one of Canada's "Top 100 Lobbyists" by the Hill Times newspaper. In 2010, Williams received CSAE's Griner Award for business excellence in the association sector. Mr. Williams holds a Masters of Business Administration from the University of Ottawa and a Bachelor of Arts (Political Science) from the University of Calgary. He has also completed studies at the Université de Tours in France.

If you have any questions or comments, please feel free to contact Huw by email at huw@impactcanada.com.

CSAE wishes to thank the following corporate sponsors
for their support

CONTENT
MANAGEMENT
Corp.

THE GLOBE AND MAIL

MORNEAU SOBECO

 RBC Royal Bank®